Perspectives on Death and Dying

Other Health & Social Care books from M&K include:

Nurses and Their Patients:
Informing practice through psychodynamic insights
ISBN: 978-1-905539-31-4 · 2009

Research Issues in Health and Social Care
ISBN: 978-1-905539-20-8 · 2009

Identification and Treatment of Alcohol Dependency
ISBN: 978-1-905539-16-1 · 2008

The Clinician's Guide to Chronic Disease Management for Long Term Conditions:
A cognitive-behavioural approach
ISBN: 978-1-905539-15-4 · 2008

The ECG Workbook
ISBN: 978-1-905539-14-7 · 2008

Routine Blood Results Explained 2/e
ISBN: 978-1-905539-38-3 · 2007

Improving Patient Outcomes
ISBN: 978-1-905539-06-2 · 2007

The Management of COPD in Primary and Secondary Care
ISBN: 978-1-905539-28-4 · 2007

Issues in Heart Failure Nursing
ISBN: 978-1-905539-00-0 · 2006

Perspectives on Death and Dying

Edited by
June L. Leishman

Perspectives on Death and Dying
June Leishman

ISBN: 978-1-905539-21-5

First published 2009

British Library Cataloguing in Publication Data
A catalogue record for this book is available from the British Library

Notice
Clinical practice and medical knowledge constantly evolve. Standard safety precautions must be followed, but, as knowledge is broadened by research, changes in practice, treatment and drug therapy may become necessary or appropriate. Readers must check the most current product information provided by the manufacturer of each drug to be administered and verify the dosages and correct administration, as well as contraindications. It is the responsibility of the practitioner, utilising the experience and knowledge of the patient, to determine dosages and the best treatment for each individual patient. Any brands mentioned in this book are as examples only and are not endorsed by the Publisher. Neither the publisher nor the authors assume any liability for any injury and/or damage to persons or property arising from this publication.

The Publisher
To contact M&K Publishing write to:
M&K Update Ltd · The Old Bakery · St. John's Street
Keswick · Cumbria CA12 5AS
Tel: 01768 773030 · Fax: 01768 781099
publishing@mkupdate.co.uk
www.mkupdate.co.uk

Designed and typeset in 11pt Usherwood Book by Mary Blood
Printed in England by Reed's Printers, Penrith

Contents

Acknowledgements

I would like to thank my two contributing authors. Without them this would be a soliloquy based on my own views and experiences; but they have endorsed my views and validated my thinking and, more importantly, enriched discussion both within the book and in the informal talks that took place as it progressed. I would also like to thank S. Maria Hampshire, for her copy-editing skills, her positive support, sound advice and encouragement.

About the authors

Professor Catherine Di Domenico PhD MA (Hons) Post Grad Dip Ed

Professor Di Domenico is Professor of Social Development and Director of Postgraduate Research Degrees in the School of Social and Health Sciences at the University of Abertay Dundee in Scotland. She was previously a senior lecturer in the Department of Sociology at the University of Ibadan, Nigeria. She is a sociologist with research interests in social development studies, especially those that focus on Africa and human rights issues. Her other research interests include gender and women's studies, tourism, rural and community studies, biographies and local histories. She has conducted research in Nigeria, in Rwanda, and in Scotland. Her work has been published in peer-reviewed journals, books, monographs and various reports. She also presents regularly at national and international conferences, with several publications in refereed conference proceedings. Her teaching interests include sociological theory, research methods, human rights, the sociology of gender, and the sociology of leisure and tourism. She also taught sociology and social psychology to nursing degree students for many years.

Dr June L. Leishman PhD Med (Hons) Post Grad Dip Ed. Cert HE Psychology Cert HE Social Psychology RMN RCNT RNT

Dr Leishman is currently Director of Operations in the School of Social and Health Sciences at the University of Abertay Dundee. She has a PhD in Social Sciences and Health as well as an Honours Masters Degree in Education. She is a registered nurse, a registered clinical nurse educator and a registered nurse teacher. Prior to her academic career, she worked with a diverse range of client groups across many different clinical settings. She has published in peer-reviewed professional journals and presented at professional conferences around the world. She helps deliver training in the areas of death and dying, research methods, and health-care education and practice. Dr Leishman has undertaken a COSCA-accredited CRUSE course in bereavement and loss. She is a Winston Churchill Fellow, a Florence Nightingale Scholar and, for services to nurse education, was invited to become a member of Sigma Theta Tau International Lambda Phi Chapter in 2005.

Dr James Moir PhD MEd (Hons) BEd

Dr Moir is currently the Director of Academic Programmes in the School of Social and Health Sciences at the University of Abertay Dundee. Dr Moir is a sociologist with a research interest in the application of discourse analysis– the analysis of the construction of "objects" in spoken, written and visual texts. He has explored diverse topics, including: the construction of occupational identities in conversation, particularly in relation to nursing and health care occupations; the doctor–patient interaction and shared decision-making; reading "body language"; representations of the "mind" in film and television; "responsibility" in relation to environmental concerns; representations of "opinions" in political polling; gender and work–life balance; and the construction of "child development" in terms of how children talk. A recurring theme across this work is examination of discursive psychology, how people relate an "inner world" of mind to an "outer world" that requires to be perceived and understood.

About this book

This book is targeted at general practitioners, hospice and care-home managers, registered nurses, social workers and counsellors, as well as anyone undertaking more focused postgraduate studies in related areas of end-of-life and palliative care. Students of the social sciences, sociology and health psychology may find it useful, as might those involved in professional education in health and social care. In addition, the book has much to offer people without a professional background, but who have an interest in the topic as a whole or specific issues.

The chapters are arranged so that readers can find relevant topics. Each chapter contains a list of references and research papers, which will help readers to extend their knowledge of available literature. We encourage all our readers to read around each topic in order to gain a broader understanding of the issues.

Preface

E noi tutti morire
"And we shall all die"

There is no getting away from the fact that death happens. It is also true to say that as a society we do not encounter dying people in ways that our predecessors did; and when we do it is generally at a later stage in our lives than our ancestors. Two social factors play a significant part in this. Firstly, we have a lowering of infant mortality rates in the UK and an increase in life expectancy, with a steady fall in death rates for both men and women (Office of National Statistics, 2007). Such changes are largely due to the social climate and social changes at any given period of time. Social unrest, increased developments in medicine and health care, as well as lifestyle choices, play a significant part in these trends. The second social factor that impacts on our encounter with dying people is the medicalisation of death.

In many households, dying and death now lie in the domain of the medical profession. Despite the preference for home as a *dying place* for many people, in modern Western society individuals most frequently die in hospitals, nursing homes and hospices. Historically there were few alternatives as to where a person ended their life. As a society we would have cared for dying relatives at home, and we would have commonly had personal experience of death at a much earlier age – with dying parents, siblings and grandparents,

However, despite a satisfactory level of published material related to terminal illness and palliative care, and the excellent training provided for those working in these specialist areas, research has identified that end-of-life and death education in health and social care education *per se* are dealt with poorly and inconsistently across all professions and at all levels.

This book does not pretend to be comprehensive. The topic is too great in scope and too complex for that. Rather, the book is designed to enhance interest in death and dying as an aspect of human life and, as such, its impact on society as a whole.

A case is made for revising death education for health-care professionals so that it takes a more comprehensive approach to this important aspect of training. Discourses drawn on within the chapters of this book will provide insights into the complexities, and some of the mysteries, that surround this area.

Each of the chapters begins with a piece of poetry or prose that readers are invited to reflect upon; and each chapter ends with a set of reflective questions relating to the chapter content that allow the reader to explore the material a little further and to consider certain issues more deeply and at a more personal level.

Chapter 1

Introduction

June L. Leishman

When I am dead, my dearest
Sing no sad songs for me
From *Song* by Christina Georgina Rossetti (1830–1894)

Death comes in many guises. It can be a still-birth or a natural end to the life trajectory. It can be the result of illness, an accident or trauma, or it can be inflicted on oneself or perpetrated by another. It can occur as a result of a natural disaster, or war or conflict, and can be enacted by individuals for a whole host of reasons – personal, social, economic and religious. It can also be the result of new pandemics such as HIV infection and AIDS, SARS, hepatitis C virus (HCV) infection and HCV-related chronic disease, or the influenza virus, or existing health challenges such as cancer and other chronic or life-threatening illnesses.

This book focuses attention on the complexity of the topics of death and dying by drawing on the interrelationship between the discourses of health, science, social anthropology, history and the social sciences. It explores some of the complexities within these domains and provides insights into the challenges faced by those who work with people who are dying or those who have experienced loss through death.

This book is not intended to be a description of "what to do" when caring for someone who is dying; rather it offers an exploration of death and dying as human conditions that impact on the person, their significant others and those involved with their care and well-being throughout this time. It is a reminder of the complex interweaving of social relationships that grows up around a dying person and how that interweaving contributes to the equally complex tapestry that is life. It is a reminder that life is itself complex, fragile and unpredictable and that dying is more than a result of illness, trauma or the natural death that occurs at the end of life (Charmaz, 1980). It also provides a flavour of the various cultural, socio-economic, environmental, political, religious, spiritual and anthropological factors that have notably influenced death and dying from before the Victorian era of "celebrating death" to the present day (Curl Stevens, 2000). As such, the reader is introduced to the way in which these factors have manipulated various practices, values and beliefs over time and how they have contributed to the attitudes towards death and dying that exist today.

As the book unfolds, the complexity of this subject becomes more apparent and provides insights into what is often, for some, a "taboo" subject. Emphasis is placed on the personal nature of death and dying, how dying is unique to the dying person and equally unique to us as individuals in terms of our attitudes, values and beliefs.

In so doing, this book may assist in understanding death and dying better, which in itself may help many professionals in their work at such times. Those with a non-professional interest may "dip" into relevant topics and will gain a broader understanding of salient issues related to death, dying and loss by reading further. This introductory chapter begins with some discussion about death itself, how it is defined and understood, the complexity of the topic and the challenges it brings to our thinking and understanding.

Defining death

Defining death

Defining death is a complex matter, one that raises much legal, ethical and medical debate (Jones, 1999). Prior to advances in resuscitation and medical technology, human death was primarily understood and diagnosed by cardiopulmonary criteria: breathing ceases, there is no pulse and the heart stops. Without the heart and lungs functioning, all other parts of the body cease to function. For generations, death was determined on the basis of the confirmed and persistent absence of these vital signs.

However, with developments in medicine, biotechnology and

transplantation, individual perceptions and the way in which death is clinically defined appear to have been challenged; accounts of methods of resuscitation have a history that can be traced back to Egyptian times. In 1767 the Dutch Humane Society published guidelines to assist the recovery of victims of drowning which advised the person undertaking the resuscitation to "keep the victim warm, give mouth-to-mouth ventilation, and perform insufflation of smoke of burning tobacco into the rectum" (Varon and Fromm, 1993). In contrast, Auger (2000) describes a case in Italy in 1774 where electric shock was used for the first time to resuscitate a "dead man".

In those days, such attempts to "bring back the dead" brought panic to members of the public, as one might expect. People began to question whether they had "prematurely buried" their loved ones, or "buried them alive". When resuscitation attempts failed, further tests were carried out to ensure that death had actually occurred. These included holding a mirror, a candle or feather to the nose and mouth to determine whether breathing was still taking place, submerging the body in water and watching for bubbles that would signify breathing, putting a bowl of liquid on their chest, or severing an artery to see if their blood "flowed" (Auger, 2000). Only after ascertaining that there was no response to these tests, would death then be pronounced by a medical practitioner.

Modern-day developments now allow us to keep people "alive" by means of assisted ventilation and heart bypass machines and with these techniques the concept of "brain death" was introduced. The first published paper on this new syndrome was presented at the Conference of the Medical Royal Colleges in 1976. Later the more accurate term "brain stem death" was coined (Byrne and Nigles, 1993). Thus the definition of death became "the irreversible cessation of all integrated functioning of the human organism as a whole, mental or physical" (Jones, 1999).

Dying is described by Kellehear (2007), as an interpersonal journey that frequently involves material, religious, financial, medical and family preparations, and he espouses the theory that people have still to recognise the fact that the dying behaviours that are exhibited by people today have been built up over thousands of years. Without medical definitions, death becomes more difficult to define. We speak of people experiencing a "living death" when we refer to those in a coma, or those who have advanced dementia (Weinstein, 2008). Doka and Aber (2002) suggest "psychological death" is the loss of what makes us who we are as a person; it is often associated with drug dependency or mental illness. An increased understanding about death – beyond the definition above – will unfold as you read through this book. Life can be viewed as a journey; death and the dying process can in fact be seen in much the same way, whether the journey is short or long.

Death trajectories

Death trajectories

Death can involve a long illness with pain and sometimes with the dependency that accompanies this, as well as the knowledge that the illness is terminal. Death can also occur quickly and with no prior knowledge that it will occur. Mortality differences, both *between* and *within* societies, are considerable. Seale (2000) cites the key features as rising life expectancy, with the resultant rise in the ageing population, coupled with the changing pattern of diseases causing death, which affect both gender and class. Therefore old age and its concomitant disabilities feature highly in the new demographic of death, but not *exclusively*. There are huge variations worldwide, and this limits the global application of Western models of terminal, or palliative care (Seale, 2000). It is considered that the shift from infectious to degenerative diseases, coupled with advances in the medical ability to predict death at an early stage (in some illnesses) have led to what we now recognise as being terminal illness around which hospice and palliative care has been developed (Hull and Jones, 1986).

For those who have been diagnosed with a terminal illness (and their families), knowing how long they will live before death finally occurs, and how much longer they might live if they comply with the medical and care regimen offered to them, are some of the key questions that they want answered.

Glaser and Strauss (1965) first described the concept of "death trajectories" in their qualitative research on death and dying in the

1960s. They noted that the temporal pattern of the disease process leading to a person's death had a profound impact on the experience of the dying person, their families and health-care professionals They also recognised that such disease trajectories could assist health-care professionals in caring for chronically ill patients. According to Glaser and Strauss (1965) the concept of a "death trajectory" is helpful in conveying to patients and families what they can expect as an illness progresses or when trauma has occurred, and it sets a common context for anticipating potential challenges and how these can be planned for. Their research was developed to make a case for changing and improving medical and health care for the dying. The recommendations they propose in their study include the amplification and deepening of education and training for health-care professionals, facilitating increased understanding of the psychological, social and organisational aspects of terminal care, promoting awareness and care planning for the "carers" of dying patients as their illness takes them in and out of the hospital environment and, finally, encouraging health professionals to engage in public discussion regarding controversial aspects of end-of-life care, such as medication prescribing regimens and issues related to prolonging life. Examples of these trajectories are illustrated in Fig 1.1.

Death trajectories go beyond depicting the physiological unfolding of a disease. They also encompass the total organisation of interprofessional involvement with the dying person and their family over the course of the illness, and the impact this has on the individuals involved. This includes the physical and emotional care undertaken by those who care for the dying person and indeed the contribution that the dying person can make to their own care throughout this period. Within "life-course" theory (Price *et al.*, 2000), trajectories – as well as "transitions" and "turning points" – are also core concepts. Trajectories are sequences or long-term patterns within a focal area, in this case dying and death. They are not individual events in time but are embedded in social pathways that are defined by social institutions and relationships that provide social support. An understanding of these trajectories may be useful to both families and individual health-care professionals near the end of life. Although they were presented by Glaser and Strauss in the late

Perspectives on death and dying

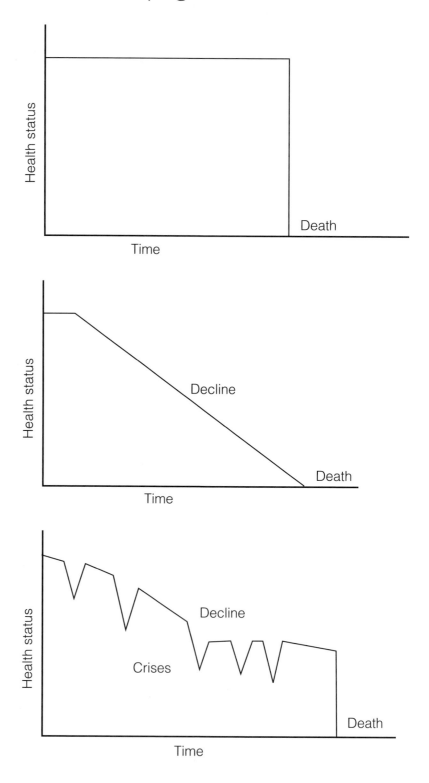

Fig 1.1. **Some examples of death trajectories**

1960s, from the viewpoint of death in hospitals and death following illness, death trajectories are still used as models in contemporary end-of-life care.

Death over the years

Death over the years

From a historical perspective, it is evident that the care of the dying and the dead has changed significantly – culturally, religiously and socially. Auger (2000) discusses how death and the disposal of the dead have been important aspects of life for all people from different eras. This is clearly shown in ancient Egypt, whereby each person had a particular aspect of care to perform for the dead, such as embalmers and undertakers who removed the body from the house and prepared it for burial. However, in Greek culture, embalming was not carried out, but perfumes and spices were rubbed on the body to mask any odours before burial; family and friends chose specific colours and types of flowers to represent the relationship they had with the deceased. Later in Greek history, cremations were carried out, as a way "to set free" the soul of the deceased (Curl Stevens, 2000).

Before the Middle Ages, taken here as the era between the 5th century and the beginning of the 16th century, it was evident that people were becoming increasingly aware of their own mortality, and the need to take responsibility for the events following their own death (Auger, 2000). Death and dying throughout that period has often been described as being connected with society and public life. Death, and the process of dying, was often thought to be a "public event". Dying people died in the presence of their families, friends and neighbours; society worked together to manage the whole process of caring for the dying and the dead (Davies, 2005).

The influential French historian, Phillipe Aries, drew on his extensive knowledge of death and dying in order to give a description of the attitudes to death held by people in the Western world. His work ranged from the time-frame of the early Middle Ages to the late 20th century (Jupp and Gittings, 1999). Aries concluded that within Christian communities, the public nature of death and dying (and the fact that it was a communal event, with society itself managing death and the aftermath, and death being understood as the transition to eternal life) meant it should be seen as a "tame death". He contrasted "tame death" with his notion of an "invisible death" which evolved over the years as a result of the shift from community and family to individualism and a society in which death was no longer experienced for the most part at home within the community or family network. This social history perspective is of value when exploring the concept of end-of-life care and the challenges that professionals face in providing high-quality health care, where not only the physical and psychological aspects of care but also the social and spiritual elements of care are important.

Death within Western society is mainly set within a medical framework. The dying are cared for by and large by medically trained people. The task of establishing that death has occurred and the "declaration of death" are the remit of the medical professional, and ascertaining the cause of death requires, in almost all cases, a medically identifiable cause, regardless of how the death actually occurred and whether or not it was predicted or intended (Davies, 2005).

However, medical definitions of death may well determine that the physical body is no longer living, but they do not answer the complex philosophical question "What is death?". There are those who question whether the death of a person is rightly understood from a solely biological viewpoint. Some of the abstract metaphysical questions that surround death present us with moral, ethical and religious dilemmas and ask us to consider the status of those whose brain functions are being maintained artificially. We are faced with questions about death being an "end in itself" or a "means to another place" where the belief in a life after death, as viewed by many religions and cultures, features strongly. Each culture has its own view on what life after death means.

Defining death as "the end of life" further fuels debate on the concept of when life begins, and it also encourages us to consider the question of death *before* birth. It also brings into focus individual human rights issues in relation to choices about how and where someone dies and what should happen with human tissues and bodies when death does occur.

Thus, it is clear that setting criteria for death is problematic. Barry (2007) categorises three areas of philosophical curiosity in relation to this issue:

1. The nature of death, including questions about consciousness, fear and evil of death.

2. Survival of death, including questions about the self and its relation to death as well as various beliefs and their bases.

3. Voluntary death, including questions about suicide, euthanasia and futile medical treatment.

Aspects of these curiosities will be addressed in the following chapters.

Conclusions

There are no clear and definitive answers to the numerous questions relating to death and dying. For many people, they will remain simply "curiosities". The discussions that follow will allow you to engage in a process of self-reflection, knowledge development and insightful understanding with regard to the complexity of death and dying. The book is not intended to change opinions or to force ideas on its readers. Rather it is hoped that it will stimulate a different way of thinking about death and dying, which may contribute to looking more thoughtfully at what for some are "big issues".

The following chapter explores issues around the fear and loneliness of dying, and introduces some coping strategies that can assist people facing death as a means of dealing with their fears and anxieties. As a society we have journeyed over the years from acceptance to discomfort and then denial of death. Chapter 2 encourages reflection on some of the philosophical curiosities relating to death and dying. These include the social construction of the meaning of death, the fear of death and how individuals cope with that fear. Chapter 3 explores death, dying and the dead body from a sociological–historical viewpoint, recognising the differences between *and* across societies, cultures and social groupings. In exploring the historical shifts that have taken place in our society in the last century to the present day, Chapter 3 provides insights into advances in knowledge as well as the changing composition of society in terms of age and ethnicity.

This is followed logically by Chapter 4 which takes a sociological stand, and presents a critical discussion on what the author proposes is a "Western language of dying", one that is firmly rooted in treating people as psychological agents. He identifies competing discourses on the "right way" to die and how to react to dying. He notes that there is now a field of thought that claims a post-modern approach to grief in terms accepting that it is a matter of individual reaction – that displays of emotion might "work" for some people, but not others; that forgetting is best for some people and remembering is best for others (Hunt, 2005). Thus Chapter 4 highlights how death brings about discursive dilemmas, namely that there is a language of how we *confront* it and also a language of how we *react* to it.

Chapter 5 highlights how, as a society, lifestyle choices affect our health and therefore contribute to heath challenges which can bring about early or unnecessary death. Chapter 6 considers hospices as "dying places" and looks briefly at the historical developments of hospices and palliative care, with reference to the UK Government's new End-of-Life Care Strategy (Department of Health, 2008).

Emphasis is placed on the elderly in Chapter 7, to examine the challenges that this age group present in relation to death, dying and bereavement and how death and dying impact on them as individuals and as a social group within society. This chapter highlights the need for age-related end-of-life care and proposes that education and training are needed for professionals and lay carers with regard to the specific needs of the elderly, wherever they are placed at the ending of their life.

A case is made in Chapter 8 for a more robust and comprehensive approach to death education for health-care professionals, incorporating discussion on spiritual care and communication skills, and presenting a model of death education that embraces the complexity of this area of study and practice. It provides scope for thinking creatively about teaching this highly sensitive subject.

This book could not possibly cover all the complex and diverse issues surrounding death and dying. There are other areas that some readers may wish to explore further; and some readers may wish to seek a different perspective on certain issues they are familiar with.

Introduction

Throughout this book, readers are encouraged to reflect on the carefully chosen extracts of poetry and prose; the same goes for the questions that appear at the end of each chapter.

References and further reading

Auger, J.A. (2000). *Social Perspectives on Death and Dying*. Halifax, Fernwood Publishing.

Barry, V. (2007). *Philosophical Thinking about Death and Dying*. Belmont, CA, Thomson Wadsworth; p. 6.

Byrne, P.A. and Nigles, R.G. (1993). The brain stem in brain death: A critical review. *Issues in Law and Medicine*, 9(1), 3–21.

Charmaz, C. (1980). *The Social Reality of Death*. Massachusetts, Addison Wesley.

Curl Stevens, J. (2000). *The Victorian Celebration of Death*. Gloucestershire, Sutton Publishing.

Davies, D.J. (2005). *A Brief History of Death*. Oxford, Blackwell Publishing.

Department of Health (2008). *End-of-Life Care Strategy*. London, Department of Health.

Doka, K.J. and Aber, R.A. (2002). Psychological loss and grief. In: K.J. Doka (ed.) *Disenfranchised Grief: New Directions, Challenges, and Strategies for Practice*. Champaign, IL, Research Press.

Glaser, B.G. and Strauss, A.L. (1965). *Awareness of Dying*. Chicago, Adline.

Hull, T.H. and Jones, G.W. (1986). Introduction: international mortality trends and differentials. In: *Consequences of Mortality Trends and Differentials*. New York, United Nations. pp. 1–9.

Hunt, S. (2005). *The Life Course: A Sociological Introduction*. Basingstoke, Palgrave.

Jones, D.A. (1999). *The UK Definition of Death. The Linacre Centre for Healthcare Ethics*. Available at: http://www.linacre.org/death.html (last accessed February 2009).

Jupp, P.C. and Gittings, C. (eds) (1999). *Death in England. An Illustrated History*. Manchester, Manchester University Press.

Katalin, H., Szanto, K., Gildengers, A., *et al.* (2002). Identification of suicidal ideation and prevention of suicidal behaviour in the elderly. *Drugs and Aging*, 19(1), 11–24.

Kellehear, A. (2007). *A Social History of Dying*. Cambridge, Cambridge University Press; p. 16.

Price S.J., McKenry, P.C. and Murphy, M.J. (eds) (2000). *Families Across Time: A Life Course Perspective*. Los Angeles, Roxbury Press.

Seale, C. (2000). *Constructing Death: The Sociology of Dying and Bereavement*. Cambridge, Cambridge University Press.

Varon J. and Fromm, R.E. (1993). Cardiopulmonary resuscitation – New and controversial techniques. *Postgraduate Medicine*, 93, 235–42.

Weinstein, J. (2008). *Working with Loss, Death and Bereavement: A Guide for Social Workers*. London, Sage Publications; p. 3.

Chapter 2
The loneliness of dying
June L. Leishman

The summons of death comes to us all, and no-one can die for another. Every one must fight his own battle with death by himself, alone. We can shout into another's ears, but everyone must himself be prepared for the time of death, for I will not be with you then, nor you with me.

Martin Luther (1483–1546)

Introduction

While death is commonly regarded as the expected end of everyone's life trajectory, people are seldom prepared for death, and few if any, seriously contemplate the idea of dying (Kubler-Ross, 1969; Armstrong-Coster, 2004; Norouzieh, 2005). Nor is there much understanding of death trajectories in the way that we understand that life follows a course of time and experience. As human beings, we are unique among the inhabitants of the earth in that we are beings with emotions and feelings. As such it is reasonable that we are touched by the death of someone close to us or the thought of our own death. From the rather practical existential philosophical perspective, we will all face death at some point in our lives. An extension to this philosophical realism is phenomenology, the study of "the thing itself"; in this case the "thing" is death and dying.

This chapter approaches thinking about death and dying by encouraging reflection on what death means in today's society. It acknowledges that for many there is a "fear" of dying and that dying can be a lonely experience; it recognises that this experience of loneliness is different for every individual. And following the introduction to the fear and loneliness of death, this chapter introduces the reader to different mechanisms employed by individuals to cope with the physical, social, spiritual, emotional and psychological needs and concerns of facing death.

Death and individual meaning

Death and individual meaning

Death means different things not only to people of different cultures, but also to people of the same culture. Death can also be approached from different perspectives, namely the "When?", "What?" and "Why?" of death, a diversity that complicates efforts to define or understand death (Kastenbaum, 2001). Beyond the medical definitions of death (which were touched on in Chapter 1) and medicalisation of death (which will appear in later chapters) the meaning of death as something more than simply a biological process has been the focus of study across a number of disciplines. A key feature of people's explanations of death has been the tension between religious and scientific views. While religious and medical explanations often coexist, it is when a person dies that personal beliefs and value systems become more acute. Seale (1995) posits that in a deeply religious society, where exposure to other forms of belief are limited, explanations of death as being "the will of God" may be comforting in promoting social acceptance of death. Psychologists studying this topic have adopted a "cradle to grave" developmental exploration of the topic from a range of perspectives (Dickinson, 1992; Wass, 1995; Kastenbaum, 2001).

Anthropologists – in particular cultural anthropologists – explore emotional responses to death in different cultures, from the preparation of the body to its final disposal (Ramsden, 1991). What these studies affirm is that death does not occur in a vacuum but rather in a social milieu. Dying is a shared experience because it has an influence on others, on close family members, on carers or on members of a society. At the same time dying people are influenced by their environment and people around them. Within the social approach, Max Weber (1964) defined social action as human behaviour to which the individual attaches subjective meaning and that takes into account the behaviour of others. As such the dying person may be influenced by what people say to them or what they *avoid* talking about. They may allow the dying person to do things for themselves, or assist with or take over doing things for the dying individual. They may respond to thinking about an after-life, if that is their belief. They may think about the length of time people visit them, or the reasons people give for *not* visiting. They may react to the tone of voice of the person speaking to them, the reactions of others to their situation, and many more factors. Therefore the "social world" of the dying person becomes a reality that gives meaning both to their living and their dying.

The objective reality of death, the biological process that occurs when someone dies, is very different from the individual's subjective experience of death. Death for many is the end of the person's world and the demise of their existence. The place where a person dies also gives meaning to death. When someone comes to realise their situation and that death is the ultimate outcome, the way that they define the situation in which their life will end has an important part to play in their dying. Dying in a hospital, a nursing home or a hospice is different from dying at home, in your own bed, in familiar surroundings and with the support of a family. Institutional settings can be viewed positively, which will help with coping behaviours. But, if the dying person feels alone or uneasy in his or her environment, then the experience of dying may be very different (Leming, 1979/80).

Meanings are created by individuals within the social and cultural world that they live in at any given period of time. Meanings change over time. As such, our 21st-century meaning may be quite unlike that of our predecessors, not least because of advances in our health and lifestyles, medical care and longevity, and the advancement of knowledge and understanding.

Fear of dying

Fear of dying

As noted above, cultural anthropologists will, as a result of their research, tell us about the many cultures that approach death without fear. There are notable individuals who have approached their own death with no apparent demonstration of fear, such as the renowned psychologist B.F. Skinner (1966); a few weeks before his death from leukaemia at the age of 86 he stated "I will be dead in a few months, but it hasn't given me the slightest anxiety or worry or anything. I always knew I was going to die". It is accepted that in a surprising number of cultures, fear is common in death-related situations. As with death itself, fear of death is an individual phenomenon, constructed and experienced differently by different people. Leming's (1979/80) Model of Death Anxiety is shown in Table 2.1, in which eight types of fear are identified and applied to either the death of self or the death of others. In his survey of over 1000 people the results of Leming's study showed that it was the *process* of dying that caused the most anxiety, rather than the *event* of death.

Table 2.1 **Eight dimensions of death anxiety as they relate to death of self or death of others (Leming, 1979/80)**

Self	Others
Process of dying	
1. Fear of dependency	Fear of financial burdens
2. Fear of pain in dying process	Fear of going through the painful experience of others dying
3. Fear of indignity in dying process	Fear of not being able to cope with physical problems of others
4. Fear of loneliness, rejection and isolation	Fear of being unable to cope emotionally with the problems of others
5. Fear of leaving loved ones	Fear of losing loved ones
State of being dead	
6. Afterlife concerns	Afterlife concerns
Fear of unknown	Fear of judgement of others – What are they thinking?
Fear of spirit world	Fear of ghosts, spirits, devils, etc.
Fear of nothingness	Fear of never seeing the person again
7. Fear of the finality of death	Fear of the end of a relationship
Fear of not being able to achieve one's goals	Guilt for not having done enough for the deceased
Fear of possible end of physical and symbolic identity	Fear of not seeing the person again
Fear of the end of all social relationships	Fear of losing the social relationship
8. Fear of the fate of the body	Fear of death objects
Fear of body decomposition	Fear of dead bodies
Fear of being buried	Fear of being in cemeteries
Fear of not being treated with respect	Fear of not knowing how to act in death-related situations

Like the meaning of death, fear of death is considered to be a result of societal and cultural beliefs, influenced by attitudes, experiences and the environment. Studies have been carried out to determine gender differences in fear of death (Pollak, 1979; Dattel and Neimeyer, 1990). These studies provide us with conflicting outcomes and poorly understood findings. Age-related fear of death studies have shown that older people are less anxious about death. Although not conclusive, these studies show that age alone does not account for the levels of death anxiety seen across age groups. Psychological maturity also features in the outcome of such studies (Rasmussen and Brems, 1996; Fortner and Neimeyer, 1999). The negative effects of horror films, grim and gruesome fairytales and myths, and historical accounts ofgrave robbers and people being buried alive have all at some time been thought to contribute to a person's fear of death and dying. Religious belief appears to provide solace for some people when contemplating death (Wilkins, 1996).

Death, loss and loneliness

Death, loss and loneliness

There has been significant social change in the last 50 years, not least in terms of living arrangements, family life and kinship, that may have a negative impact on individuals in terms of social isolation (Van Baarsen, 2002). Kunitz (2004) claimed that social capital – bonds between individual people and in social groups – contribute significantly to health and well-being. But the terms "loneliness" and "being alone" are not the same thing. "Alone" is a state that describes being on one's own; but loneliness is a state of mind that can occur when a person is on his or her own or in the company of others. There are many people who are *alone* but are not lonely and many who are surrounded by family and friends but experience feelings of loneliness. *Loneliness* manifests itself in many different ways. It can bring about profound physical and psychological feelings of emptiness, fear, sorrow and emotional pain – particularly acutely when facing death. Similarly, the loneliness of death and dying can be experienced in different ways by both the dying person and the bereaved. The feeling of loneliness might be described as being disconnected from others, even when they are physically present, and feeling "too different" to bridge the gap. One's suffering may be too great, or one's perspective may be too radically altered by knowledge and experience about illness and death to be shared with people who are not suffering in exactly the same way.

While loneliness *per se* is not diagnosed as an illness, the affective, cognitive and behavioural features of loneliness can be helped. Interest in the experience of loneliness grew in the 1970s and 1980s across a range of disciplines and from a number of perspectives, mainly with respect to age or socially disadvantaged groups (Van Baarsen, 2002). In relation to loneliness and death and dying, Rokach *et al.* (2007) compared the manner in which dying people, their carers and their families cope with loneliness. Friedman (2000) explored the experience of loneliness among young adult cancer patients. Cherry and Smith (1993) analysed the narratives of men diagnosed with AIDS in order to illustrate the accepted typology of loneliness in their stories, these being social isolation, emotional isolation and existential isolation. Research into loneliness has also included cultural studies (Sarhill *et al.*, 2001) and sibling bereavement (Forward and Garlie, 2003). New research examines loneliness as experienced by the elderly. Loneliness does not respect any boundaries of age, gender, culture or health status. It is a universal phenomenon. It is also multidimensional, varying in intensity depending on the cause and situation.

Despite current research interest, it is clear from the literature that this area of study remains a work in progress. As individual people experience death and dying in their lives, the fear of dying and loss of self and social existence becomes a monumental trigger for the experience of loneliness and all its manifestations. How someone copes with this is again manifest at a personal level. Later in the book further discussion on loneliness will be presented, with a particular focus on the elderly.

Coping with death and loss

Coping with death and loss

When faced with a significant life event, people mobilise untaught coping mechanisms to deal with the situation they find themselves in. Similarly, when faced with death or the dying experience, similar coping strategies fall into place. Coping strategies are central to the concept of *resilience*, the human capacity of all individuals to transform and change (Lifton, 1994). Coping is defined as "constantly changing cognitive and behavioural efforts to manage specific external or internal demands" (Lazarus and Folkman, 1984). However, loss challenges the ability to cope effectively and there are many different ways of coping, some more positive than others. The discussion that follows focuses among others, on the interviews of Kubler-Ross (1969) with terminally ill patients on the coping mechanisms they utilise at different stages of their illness. Corr (2000; cited in Coyle, 2006) highlights a range of physical needs and concerns that dying individuals face such as maintaining their body image and functional capacity, and the minimisation of physical distress, as being central to ways of coping with the inevitability of death. Meanwhile, Gavrin and Chapman (1995) remind us that pain is one of the most commonly experienced physical concerns, as it can contribute to several problems such as depression, helplessness and hopelessness. All of these things negatively impact on quality of end-of-life – physically, socially, emotionally and psychologically. Pain control is therefore an important coping mechanism which dying people employ. Where drug therapy is the mechanism of choice, it should be administered in dosages that enable the dying person to live a pain-free and *alert* life, as well as enabling them to retain as much control of their life as possible, so they can complete unfinished business or, as Kubler-Ross refers to it in her classic book *On Death And Dying* (1969), *drawing closure* to the many facets of their lives.

However, dying people may attempt to maximise their capacity to endure physical pain, as a way of protecting their loved ones from the harsh realities of their dying experience. Armstrong-Coster (2004) feels that this coping mechanism has a negative impact on the quality of the end-of life experience, and is supported in this claim by Johanson (1993), who aptly points out that "...unrelieved, purposeless, chronic pain leads to anxiety, depression and suffering, which in turn can accelerate the natural process of deterioration" (Cook and Oltjenbrun, 1998; p. 41).

Dying is also as much a social phenomenon as it is a physical one (Crumbie, 2007). While we are all individuals, humans are also social beings who live out our lives in the company of others;

therefore fear of *loss* of company is an important aspect that many dying people have to deal with. In their fear of being isolated, lonely, and possibly abandoned, dying people may use avoidance strategies such as deliberate silence and avoidance of issues relating to their impending death; these are attempts to push aside painful or frightening interactions (Dupee, 1982; cited in Cook and Oltjenbrun, 1998). While the motives for protecting their close family or friends by resorting to a conspiracy of silence may be positive, Cook and Oltjnenbrun (1998) point out that *open* communication about death makes room for mutual support and relief of potential, maybe irrational, fears about loneliness and abandonment, thus enabling the dying person to conclude previously unresolved issues.

Withdrawal is another coping strategy used when someone is faced with death. Surprisingly, Evans and Potts (2002) view the emotional distancing associated with withdrawal as a positive coping mechanism, particularly as an illness progresses. This, they claim, is due to the fact that dying individuals may not have adequate physical and/or psychological energy to maintain a large circle of relationships. Therefore they may require time to draw closure to most aspects of their lives, as well as wait for the ultimate end (Charmaz, 1980).

Dying people also need to cope with the psychological, spiritual and emotional distress associated with facing death. This psychological distress generally manifests itself as general feelings of hopelessness, helplessness, depression, anxiety, demoralisation, or – in extreme cases – a desire to hasten death. All of these are common reactions of somebody facing death (McClain *et al.*, 2003). Spirituality, on the other hand, is the way in which people understand their lives or existence in view of their ultimate meanings and values (Muldoon and King, 1995; Mitchell, 2008). For many dying people, traditional expressions of their faith, such as prayer, the sacraments, or visits from a chaplain or faith leader, give them great comfort. Although many turn to religion at this time, others find support through their spiritual beliefs outside the context of organised religion (Coyle, 2006; Mitchell, 2008). Growing evidence from empirical studies supports the hypothesis that spiritual well-being is a central component of psychological and emotional health for anyone facing death. Moreover, the ability to find or sustain meaning in one's life during a terminal illness might help to deter end-of-life despair more significantly than spiritual well-being that is rooted in a religious faith (Coward, 1988; cited in McClain *et al.*, 2003; Mitchell, 2008;). Spiritual well-being is becoming increasingly recognised as a buffer against the helplessness and hopeless-ness associated with a life devoid of meaning, and, as such, an important coping mechanism for individuals facing death (McClain *et al.*, 2003). The dying person can mobilise one coping mechanism, use more than one coping mechanism at any time, employ a combination of mechanisms, or switch back and forth in their choice of mechanism, depending on the presenting challenges at different stages of illness (Charles-Edwards, 2005).

Denial is typically an initial reaction to the diagnosis of a terminal illness. The dying individual disputes the bad news, preferring to believe that it cannot be happening to him or herself (Kubler-Ross, 1969; Weisman, 1976). Denial functions as a buffer that allows the dying person to recuperate from the shock of the diagnosis. It also enables them to maintain some sense of composure while adapting to the stresses and pressures of facing death. It also shields them from the realities of their condition, not only during the first stages but also at various stages in their illness trajectory (Noruzieh, 2005). It is important to note that denial is employed not only to avoid reality, but also to confirm reality, for example, as when they wish to delay death so that they can continue to enjoy the pleasures of life within the context of their imminent death. However, persistent denial can be counter-productive, especially with the obvious progression of terminal illness, hence the role of other more appropriate coping mechanisms (Rose *et al.*, 1997).

Anger – characterised by the "Why me?" type of questioning – is another coping mechanism that dying people employ as they "ease out" of their initial denial (Kubler-Ross, 1969). This may be directed at the environment, at their God, at close relations, or even at health-care professionals (Noruzieh, 2005). Expressions of anger as a coping mechanism can result in isolation, loneliness, and even abandonment, where significant others find interactions with the dying person unbearable. This negatively impacts on the quality of their end-of-life. However, Noruzieh (2005) points out that the expression of anger can have a calming effect, and therefore can be beneficial.

It is at times such as these that some people may also bargain secretly with their God to postpone their death (Cook and Oltjenbrun, 1998). Bargaining is often mobilised in response to the dying person's irrational fears and feelings of guilt (Kubler-Ross, 1969). While eliciting such concerns could bring relief from fear, thereby enhancing end-of-life quality, such bargaining tends to be a secret coping mechanism, with an impact on quality of end-of-life that is difficult to determine. It is not uncommon for reactive depression to be experienced at some point during a person's death trajectory. This is often precipitated by the many losses they have to endure. Kubler-Ross (1969) also alerts us to preparatory depression where the dying person becomes preoccupied with what lies ahead, as opposed to his or her past. This type of depression is both necessary and beneficial as a way of enabling the person who is dying to reach a stage of acceptance, rather than facing death when they are full of regrets or resentful about leaving unfinished business behind (Kubler-Ross, 1969). It also contributes to what is known as a "good death" where the individual has thought through and planned their end-of- life.

Reminiscing is yet another coping mechanism. Reminiscing enables the person to share their valuable life contributions, or what might be described as their legacy. They are made up of core values and accomplishments that will live on after his or her death (Coyle, 2006). Reminiscence can thus be viewed as a boost to a dying person's self esteem.

According to Kubler-Ross (1969), after having the opportunity of mobilising the various coping mechanisms discussed above, most people reach a stage when they accept their ultimate end with calmness and dignity. In the final stages before death, however, Kubler-Ross suggests it may be more beneficial and worthwhile to mobilise more passive coping strategies – to let go of the struggle to live, and to accept one's death as a reality. It should be noted that acceptance of death is not necessarily universal; many dying individuals experience denial and anger right through to the end (Rose *et al.*, 1997).

It is important however to remember that different people

experience a mix of emotions at different points in time, and these emotions may peak, diminish, or recur at different times. There will be highs and lows, calling for a revival of whichever coping mechanisms best addressed the concerns and needs of those different stages (Cook and Oltjenbrun, 1998). These mixed emotions and reactions can often be confusing for the individual, their family and the health-care professionals working with them. It is a dynamic process which changes depending on the individual and their particular situation.

Hope is a coping mechanism that dying people use continually throughout their suffering, as it tends to give them a sense of a special mission in life (Kubler-Ross, 1969). This helps maintain their spirits, and enables them to endure the often stressful tests and treatment regimens that go with terminal illnesses. Hope is not always related to the anticipation of a cure. For some, it lies in the belief in an after-life, or in maintaining some form of control in their lives despite their terminal illness. For others, it manifests itself as a rationalisation for their suffering; while for others it represents some form of denial whereby they anticipate a miracle in the face of worsening symptoms (Cook and Oltjenbrun, 1998). Hope can be viewed as a *cushion* for dying individuals throughout their very difficult journey. It somehow makes the death burden bearable for both the dying and their carers.

There are a range of mechanisms that a dying person can call on when faced with death, of course, but Charles-Edwards (2005) points out a paradox here: that the harder and longer the dying person demonstrates his or her maturity may relate to how well they are able to collaborate in letting go of the independence that may have been achieved slowly since birth. This means letting go of everything one has acquired through life, accepting the fate that lies ahead, and living as best one can till the very end.

The literature suggests that from the perspective of the health-care professional, the concept of a "good" or "bad" death relates to the extent to which the individual has control over the dying process. A "good death" is often associated with a dignified end-of-life, that is peaceful, respectful and pain free. It is often associated with western philosophies of palliative care which have their origins in the early hospice movement.

Conclusions

This chapter encourages reflection on some philosophical attitudes relating to the phenomena of death and dying. It examines how meanings of death can be socially constructed, identifying some of the fears that people have about death and dying and how they are also socially and culturally constructed, providing some insight into how people employ different coping mechanisms to help with their fears and the process of dying. There are no universal answers for these complicated issues, but one overarching factor that emerges from these discussions is that this is a complex and dynamic aspect of the human condition, whereby all the issues discussed here reinforce the individuality of the experience of death and dying and the social and cultural premises on which these individual experiences are founded.

There is no doubt that many of us are ill-prepared for death. For most people, the fear of death and dying is very real. Loneliness during this period, and the need for support from close family and friends, features significantly throughout the process of dying and at the time of death for a great many people. Most dying people maintain hope throughout their end-of-life experience, but for very different reasons – in anticipation of a miraculous cure, in the hope of an extended life, of a better future, or of a legacy that endures after death. Chapter 3 will develop the debate further, looking at how social change has influenced the way we think about death and dying.

Reflective questions

1. Make a list of the losses (not just loss as a result of death) that you have experienced in your life so far. What have these losses meant to you?

2. What do you think is the difference between *defining* death and explaining the *meaning* of death?

3. The death of even a single person results in the loss of many "roles" held by that one person. Think of all of the "roles" you have and the impact that death would have on your family and friends.

4. Many people fear death and dying. What fears would you have in this situation, and why? If you have no fears, think about why that is so.

5. What is your response to the statement that "death is about more than the biological ending of life"?

References and further reading

Armstrong-Coster. A. (2004). *Living and Dying with Cancer*. Cambridge, Cambridge University Press.

Chapman (1992) Gavrin, J. and Chapman, C.R. (1995). Clinical management of dying patients. *Western Journal of Medicine* 163(3), 268–77.

Charles-Edwards. D. (2005). *Handling Death and Bereavement at Work*. London, Routledge.

Charmaz, K.C. (1980) *The Social Reality of Death*. Reading MA, Addison Wesley.

Cherry, K. and Smith, D.H. (1993). Sometimes I cry: The experience of loneliness for men with Aids. *Health Communications* 5(3), 181–208.

Cobb, M. (2002). *Facing Death: The Dying Soul*. Buckingham, Open University Press.

Cook. A.S. and Oltjenbrun, K.A. (1998). *Dying and Grieving: Lifespan and Family Perspectives*, 2nd edn. Fortworth, Harcourt Brace.

Coyle. N.C. (2006). The hard work of living in the face of death. *Journal of Pain and Symptom Management* 32(3), 266–74.

Crumbie. A. (2007). Death, grief and loss. In: M. Walsh and A. Crumbie (eds). *Watson's Clinical Nursing and Related Sciences*, 7th edn. Edinburgh, Bailliere Tindall.

Dattel, A.R. and Neimeyer, R.A. (1990). Sex differences in death anxiety: Testing the emotional expressiveness hypothesis. *Death Studies*, 14, 1–11.

Department of Health (2007). *Health profile of England 2007, 22nd October 2007* (Ref. 8755.). Available at: http://www.dh.gov.uk/en/Publicationsandstatistics/Publications/PublicationsStatistics/DH_079716] (last accessed February 2009).

Dickinson, D. and Johnson, M. (1992). *Death, Dying and Bereavement*. Milton Keynes, The Open University.

Evans, D.W. and Potts, M. (2002). Brain death. *British Medical Journal*, 325, 598.

Fortner, B.V. and Neimeyer, R.A. (1999). Death anxiety in older adults: A quantitative review. *Death Studies*, 23, 387–412.

Forward, D. and Garlie, N.W. (2003). Search for new meaning: Adolescent bereavement after the sudden death of a sibling. *Canadian Journal of School Psychology* 18(1/2), 23–53.

Friedman, W.J. (2000). Neurotrophins induce death of hippocampus neurons via the p75 receptor. *The Journal of Neuroscience*, 20(17), 6340–46.

General Register Office for Scotland (2007). *Mortality Statistics*. Available at: http://www.gro-scotland.gov.uk/statistics/deaths/index.html (last accessed February 2009).

Hanlon, P. (2005). Scots' death wish proves fatal flaw. *Sunday Times*, 9 January 2005.

Hope, J. (1990). Can there really be life after death? *Daily Mail*, 5 October 1990.

Ivan, L. and Melrose, M. (1986). *The Way We Die*. Angel Press, Chichester.

Johanson, G.A. (1993). Midazolam in terminal care. *American Journal of Hospital Palliative Care*, 10, 13–14.

Kastenbaum. R.J. (2001). *Death, Society and Human Experience*, 7th edn. Boston, Allyn and Bacon.

Kubler-Ross. E. (1969). *On Death and Dying*. London, Routledge.

Kunitz, S.J. (2004). Social capital and health. *British Medical Bulletin*, 69, 1–13.

Lazarus, R.S. and Folkman, S. (1984). *Stress, Appraisal and Coping*, New York, Springer; p. 141.

Leming, M.R. (1979/80). Religion and death: A test to Homans' theory. *Omega – Journal of Death and Dying*, 10, 347–64.

Lifton, R. (1994). *The Protean Self: Human Resilience in an Age of Fragmentation*. New York, Basic Books.

Luther, M. (1980). Eight Sermons at Wittenberg, 1522. In: *Luther's Works*, Volume. 51. Philadelphia, Fortress Press, p. 70. Translated from German by John Doberstein.

McClain. C.S., Rosenfeld B. and Breitbart, W. (2003). Effect of spiritual well-being on end-of-life despair in terminally ill cancer patients. *The Lancet* 361, May 10, 1603–07.

Mitchell, D. (2008). Spiritual and cultural issues at the end of life. *Journal of Medicine* 36(2), 109–10.

Muldoon, M. and King, N. (1995). Spirituality, health care, and bioethics. *Journal of Religion and Health*, 34(4), 329–49.

Norouzieh, K. (2005). End-of-life care: Case management of the dying child. *Journal of Medicine* 33(2), 25– 29.

Office of National Statistics (2007). *Death registrations in 2005*. Available at: http://www.statistics.gov.uk/cci/nugget.asp?id = 952 (last accessed February 2009).

Pollak, J.M. (1979). Correlates of death anxiety: A review of empirical studies. *Omega – Journal. of Death and Dying*, 10(2), 97–121.

Ramsden, I. (1991). Cultural safety. *New Zealand Nursing Journal*, 83(11), 18–19.

Rasmussen, C. and Brems, C. (1996). The relationship of death anxiety with age and psychosocial maturity. *Journal of Psychology* 130, 141–44.

Rhodes, R., Francis, L. and Silvers, A. (2007). *The Blackwell Guide to Medical Ethics*. Oxford, Blackwell.

Rokach, A., Matalon, R., Safarov, A. and Bercovitch, M. (2007). The dying, those who care for them, and how they cope with loneliness. *The American Journal of Hospice and Palliative Care*, 24(5), 399–407.

Rose. K., Webb, C. and Waters, K.((1997). Coping strategies employed by informal carers of terminally ill cancer patients. *Journal of Cancer Nursing* 1(3), 126–33.

Sabom, M. (1982). *Recollections of Death: A Medical Investigation*. Harper and Row, New York.

Sarhill, N., LeGrand, S., Islambouli, R., Davis, M.P. and Walsh, D. (2001). The terminally ill Muslim: Death and dying from the Muslim perspective. *American Journal of Hospice and Palliative Medicine*, 18(4), 251–54.

Scott, T. (1990). "Just a few months". In: H. Alexander (ed.). *Living with Dying*. London, BBC Publications.

Scottish Executive (2009). *NHS Scotland Performance Targets – Health Improvement*. Available at: http://www.scotland.gov.uk/Topics/Health/NHS-Scotland/17273/targets/Health (last accessed February 2009).

Seale, C. (1995). Dying alone. *Sociology of Health and Illness*, 17(3), 376–92.

Shaw, A., McMunn, A. and Field, J (2000). *The Scottish Health Survey, 1998*. Available at: http://www.sehd.scot.nhs.uk/scottishhealthsurvey/sh8-00.html (last accessed February 2009).

Skinner, B.F. (1966). *Science and Human Behaviour*. New York, Macmillan.

Van Baarsen, B. (2002). Theories in coping with loss. *Journal of Gerontology, Series B: Psychosocial Sciences and Social Sciences* 56, 33–42.

Wass, H. (1995). Death in the lives of children and adolescents. In: H. Wass and R.A. Neimeyer (eds) *Dying: Facing the Facts*, 3rd edn. Washington, DC, Taylor & Francis.

Weber, M. (1964). *The theory of social and economic organisation*. New York, NY, Free Press.

Weisman, A. (1976). *On Dying and Denying*. New York, Behavioural Publications.

Wells, R. (1988). *Helping Children Cope with Grief: Facing a Death in The Family*. London, Sheldon Press.

Wilkins, W. (1996). The naturalness of dying. *Journal of Occupational and Environmental Medicine*, 38(9), 867.

Chapter 3
Death, dying and the dead body
Catherine Di Domenico

Stop all the clocks, cut off the telephone,
Prevent the dog from barking with a juicy bone,
Silence the pianos and with muffled drum
Bring out the coffin, let the mourners come.

From *Funeral Blues* by W.H. Auden (1907–1973)

Introduction

How do different societies and cultures manage death, dying, and the bodies of the dead? In this chapter, sociological recognition is given to the differences between and across societies, cultures and social groups in terms of attitudes towards death, dying and the dead body. These differences are explored through a sociological–historical lens. Changes in attitudes in the UK over the 20th and 21st centuries to death, dying and the dead body reflect, in part, key historical shifts that have taken place in our society. These can be examined in terms of advances in knowledge, as well as the changing composition of society in terms of both age structures and ethnicity.

The variety of experiences of death relate to the different ages when death takes place, and this is reflected in the age structure of the society of which they are a part. Societies differ from one another in terms of their age composition, (that is, the proportion of the total population found in different age groups). This is mainly due to different mortality rates, as well as fertility and migration rates. Economically advanced societies, such as the UK, generally have a relatively low proportion of children, a large intermediate group and a relatively high proportion of older

Perspectives on death and dying

people. As a society develops economically there is usually an increase in the numbers of older people and a decrease in the numbers of children; death among children is much rarer than death among the elderly. The age distribution pattern in developed countries largely reflects a decrease in fertility rate, coupled with lower mortality among younger people. Mortality rates in low-income countries are more evenly spread throughout all age groups than in relatively high-income societies. Life for everyone in these low-income countries is less certain because of droughts, famines, wars, accidents, illnesses and infectious diseases such as AIDS and malaria, that affect people in all stages of life. However, the high death rate includes both extremely high infant and child mortality and maternal mortality rates; this was true of Great Britain in previous centuries, whereby deaths in childhood occurred but were less publicly mourned, although no less of a tragedy. Childhood deaths in poor countries are almost inevitable, and fertility rates are also higher in order to ensure that the family will have surviving children. High fertility rates are maintained among first-generation migrants to the UK from less economically advanced countries. However, they fall to the lower rate of native-born people by the second or third generation because of the impact of the cultural values of wider society on the children of ethnic minority communities.

The UK is not only a much older society in terms of age composition, but also a more multicultural society, as reflected in the diversity of our beliefs, deriving both from our own traditions and those of migrant ethnic communities. The ethnic and religious diversity of the UK in the 21st century relates to the cultural differences in the parts of the world that the migrants came from. It seems that people from minority ethnic and cultural backgrounds often do not use palliative care services as much as they might. Thus it is necessary for everyone to be aware of the diversity of cultural attitudes in the UK. This chapter explores some of the beliefs about death, dying and the dead body found among the different ethnic and religious groups who make up this vibrant population.

The chapter also examines the cultural beliefs and attitudes of our society in the widest possible sense, in terms of the emphasis on youth and different emphases on the body and the uses of dead bodies by the living that prevail in our culture today. These beliefs and attitudes affect our views on ageing and death and the use of body parts (when, for example, we consider becoming organ donors). Thus the dominant positivist or scientific cultural orientation in the West contrasts with more traditional religious belief systems in terms of dealing with the body following death, and also with the post-modern awareness of the importance of respecting different attitudes to ageing, death, dying and the body. The role of spirituality in professional care and the part holism plays in caring for the dying should also be considered.

To examine the complexity of overlapping issues pertaining to death, dying and dead bodies, this chapter is framed around six broad thematic areas. They facilitate exploration of important dimensions and debates within a coherent discursive frame. First of all, sociological perspectives on death and dying in the West are considered from a socio-historical standpoint, introducing the diverse perspectives from cultural and religious tenets. This provides a more macro-level critique and takes the work of Durkheim on religion and suicide (Durkheim 1915; 1952) as a useful starting point – a framework that is still relevant to contemporary debates on the individual's role in society. Also explored through a sociological lens and historical framework are the three ideal types of death as developed by Walter (1994; 1998) in relation to more economically advanced nations. These are the traditional, modern and neo-modern social perspectives; our focus is on the latter stage, where we are today in the UK. The discussion then examines death, dying and burial more specifically in the UK context, using a historical approach to explore attitudes relating to the British experience and cultural landscape per se. The concepts of family and culture and how these inform and intersect with everyday choices and experiences of death and dying provide another locus of discussion. Old age is also examined because our death, particularly so-called "natural" death, is an inevitable eventual outcome of the ageing process. The dead body, its treatment and its potential uses for the living, are also discussed, including exploration of death and burial practices in traditional societies, and drawing on examples from Africa about the body, death and dying, cultural awareness and uses of the dead to the living.

Sociological perspectives on death and dying

Sociological perspectives

In sociology, research on different types of modes of dying, death and burial, and how they are affected by different cultures and social structures, has not been of central interest. Historians and social anthropologists, however, have always been interested in exploring different cultural traditions associated with death and burial. Interest in this topic goes back to the work of the founding fathers, and especially Emile Durkheim, the famous French sociologist of the late 19th and early 20th centuries. Durkheim was opposed to the notion that a society was nothing more than a simple collection of individuals; rather he developed a concept of holism in which he stressed the social whole or community to which we belong, and how it affected individual choices and actions.

Durkheim looked at the various habits and practices of simpler communities, which he saw as eventually becoming traditions that were later often given religious authority. He explored different traditions and religious practices of both pre-modern and modern cultures and how they related to death, dying and burial. For example, he described the practices of Aboriginal mourners in Australia, which even involved dangerous mutilations of their own bodies (Durkheim, 1915). He also conducted a well-known study of suicide (Durkheim, 1952), showing how suicide rates in Europe had been greatly influenced by different cultural and social systems that affected the individual decision to commit suicide. Thus, suicide could be seen as a "social" and "cultural" as well as an "individual" fact. He described four types of suicide – altruistic, fatalistic, egoistic and anomic – which he found to be the result of either high or low levels of social integration, moral regulation and oppressiveness. Many of Durkheim's ideas have relevance to our understanding of cultural and social patterns which affect not only suicide rates in present-day societies but our approaches to death, dying and the dead body, which are socially and culturally influenced. It is therefore of interest to explore Durkheim's four types of suicide in greater depth in order to gain a deeper understanding of these influences.

Altruistic suicide, which is relatively rare, was the result of a very high level of social integration whereby individuals were willing to sacrifice their own lives for the social or religious group. Thus in Japan ritual suicide was preferable to dishonour. Previously among the Hindus, widows were expected to commit *suttee*, often agreeing to being burned alive on the funeral pyre of their dead husbands; these practices now rarely occur although surviving widows still have low status, which adds to their economic and emotional loss. Indeed, the altruistic assisted suicide of elderly people by their younger relatives, as well as their equally altruistic unassisted suicide, was common in the past when times were hard. This took place among Yupik and Inuit people, commonly collectively referred to as Eskimo, as well as other nomadic peoples. Altruistic suicide is relatively rare today, although terrorist suicide bombers often see themselves as religious martyrs. Most followers of Islam vehemently disagree with their interpretation of the Qur'an.

Another type of suicide – also relatively rare – is fatalistic suicide. This occurs in extremely authoritarian, oppressive societies or organisations, including prisons and detention centres. Some people prefer to take their own lives rather than live under such conditions. In contemporary Western societies, prison officers are constantly on the watch for attempted suicides, especially among new prisoners, young men, mentally ill prisoners and those who abuse drugs. Attempted suicide is particularly common among illegal immigrants and refugees who have been denied permission to stay in countries of the European Union (sometimes pejoratively called "Fortress Europe") and among those who are in detention, awaiting deportation to their country of origin – especially when that country is extremely oppressive or unstable.

Egoistic suicide occurs when there is too little social integration. Individuals are insufficiently bound into social group norms, values and goals. Unmarried males who are not integrated into family life are more likely to commit suicide than those who are married. Again Durkheim (1952) found that suicide rates were higher in countries with Protestant rather than Roman Catholic religious cultures. He postulated that Protestantism left the individual more emotionally isolated than Catholicism.

Similarly, with anomic suicide the individual feels isolated and lacks a clear sense of identity. This happens when the society does not reflect a stable set of values and standards due to rapid changes, whether they are "positive" (as in times of economic boom) or "negative" (as in a rapid economic downturn). Instability in society may also be caused by disruptions from war, conquest, revolution, or even the rapid introduction of innovative technology. Reflecting on this, Durkheim also found that there were more suicides in urban areas than in more stable rural areas, and more among members of the middle class than the working class. Young men, especially those living in the deprived urban areas of formerly industrial cities in the West, may feel very disadvantaged either when economic, political or environmental disaster strikes to effect negative changes in their lives, or when they feel that their world offers them comparatively few opportunities despite "taunting" them with desirable consumer commodities.

Despite Durkheim's classic work on suicide, little research was conducted in Western sociology on the subject of death and dying until the 1960s (in contrast to social anthropology). Geoffrey Gorer's work (1965) made an impact on the neglected field of research on death and dying in British sociology. He pointed out how, in the post-war period in which he was writing, there was no longer an emphasis on the rituals that had previously surrounded death, and that death had become a "taboo" in much the same way that sex had once been. He went as far as describing it as the "pornography of death" (1965; p. 169). Sociologists in America also gave us important insights through their research into the American experience of dying in hospital. Glaser and Strauss (1965) famously conducted groundbreaking research on the "American way of death" in a modern hospital ward, studying patients dying of cancer. Their interest was the influence of awareness on interactions with dying people, differentiating between closed awareness, suspicion, mutual deception, and open awareness. They postulated that the type of awareness that patients had would impact on their interactions in the hospital with staff as well as with friends and relatives.

Walter (1994; 1998) explores attitudes to death and dying in the West from a historical perspective. His work impacts on sociological thinking about death in our societies. He develops three logically coherent, or ideal, types of death. These are traditional, modern and neo-modern. He shows them to be deeply rooted in their respective social and cultural contexts. In the traditional context, such as small-scale communities where life expectancy is low and life itself is thought to be a preparation for an after-life, death tends to be quick, occurring frequently throughout life, and is relatively public. The authoritative force that dictates how death should be regarded and dealt with by the community and wider society comes from religious belief systems and traditions. This context gives way historically to the contrasting modern, rational, industrial, urban context – life expectancy is on average "three score years and ten", and death occurs in a hidden way, no longer within the community. Public and private contexts are separated from each other, with the authority over the process of dying being given to the medical professional, usually a doctor, and with the location of death being generally an institution, like a hospital or nursing home for the elderly. However, there may still be reliance on a traditional church funeral service before burial or cremation takes place.

The modern context in turn gives way to the present-day, neo-modern one, in which there has been a revival of interest in death. It is a much more prolonged affair, generally affecting the very old, and the private and public are more intertwined once again. Walter (1994) revealed a shift away from the traditional church funeral service to individually planned funerals in which the dying person selects their own music and poetry before they die, and a greater reliance on holistic, spiritual understanding based on personal experience and bereavement counselling. Contemporary neo-modern death is becoming more and more prominent in our thinking as we look to the future in the 21st century, and away from the modernism of the 20th century. Walter (1994) suggests two strands to our approaches to contemporary death and dying, the late-modern and the post-modern strands. He defines the late-modern strand of neo-modern death as relying on "professional expertise to promote the good death and healthy grieving" (1994; p. 202). The late-modern approach has been heavily influenced by the views of various writers such as Kubler-Ross (1969) who informs us as a professional how to cope with death. Kubler-Ross claims that individuals go through five stages of dying in terms of adjusting to the approach of death. These stages are denial, anger, negotiating a divine intervention, resignation and acceptance. Bereaved people may go through similar stages. Post-modern death, on the other hand, is that strand of neo-modern death "that acknowledges wide variability in human responses to death and loss" (1994; p. 203). The post-modern strand embraces the different ways in which people approach death in a culture that emphasises difference, individual experience and the authority of the self – but no longer supports any particular grand narrative, whether traditional such as in religion, or modern such as the belief in science and rationality. These different perspectives on death may be linked to a variety of cultural, traditional and religious practices, and even modern techniques, but they have no authority in themselves. Rather, in a rapidly changing post-modern "pick and mix" culture there is a double-coding or combining of "modern techniques with elements believed to be traditional in order to create a more consumer-friendly product or service" (Walter, 1994; p. 202).

Death and dying in the UK in historical and comparative perspectives

Death and dying in the UK

The presence of death has always been a part of all human life and culture. The UK is no exception. Indeed, especially until the economic, social, public health and medical improvements of the last century, it was routine and a generally accepted "presence" throughout British life. This has been so in this country both historically and until relatively recently, while in the less economically affluent nations of the world it is still the case. Only the very lucky citizens of these lower-income nations experience a relatively long and healthy life, like we generally do in the UK; only a minority achieve the status of elder and a "good" death at an advanced age, surrounded by family and friends. A "good" death, although an ideal in the UK, may also not always be achievable at present, where death has become more and more associated with the ageing process, which is an anathema to citizens of a nation dominated by a culture of youth. The dead body also became the object of our scientific or educational study rather than imbued with spiritual, religious and social meaning, although efforts are being made to rekindle a new type of post-modern spirituality.

In Victorian and Edwardian times in Christian Britain the funeral ceremonies and tombstones or crypts of the "great and the good" were made as elaborate as possible to show respect for the dead person. Eulogies were also read out that praised the virtues of the dearly departed. This is still the case for significant public figures in the UK who are sometimes given a ceremonial funeral, and very rarely, as in the case of the monarch, a state funeral. In many developing countries within the British Commonwealth, with population structures more like that of Victorian rather than present-day Britain, ceremonies based on the Victorian or Edwardian models were adopted by the elite when burying their venerated older citizens. They still take place today. For example, in Southern Nigeria many people run up debts in order to give a senior member of their family a "good send-off", with the custom of the "wake" being extremely popular. In the UK church attendance has declined, in contrast to Nigeria where it is on the increase, and has been accompanied by a decline in formal ritualised mourning and elaborate funeral ceremonies and an increase in more individually planned ones, such as the funeral depicted in the film *Four Weddings and a Funeral* at which W.H Auden's notable poem 'Funeral Blues' was recited. This type of individualised, post-modern funeral is becoming more popular in the UK today.

In the mid to late 20th century in the UK, the developing youth culture and the medicalisation of death separated death increasingly both physically and socially from everyday life and culture. Dying people were often removed to special hospital wards, away from family and friends. In Britain, death still tends to be a more isolated and isolating experience and far less a part of everyday life, with more people than ever dying in hospitals or nursing homes for the elderly, far away from family and friends. Indeed, in the UK at the end of the 20th century almost 70 per cent of deaths took place in hospitals (Dickinson and Johnson, 1993). In the last century in Europe, in contrast to previous centuries and other societies, the attitude in the UK has been described as "death-denying" (Aries, 1981). When death does take place, the funeral industry is there to provide a professional service to the

Perspectives on death and dying

family and to orchestrate the behaviour of the mourners outside the home, in the funeral parlour and at the graveside. The industrialisation of death in this way has resulted in most cases in a move away from the family and community – much as has happened with other aspects of family life and work.

Dominant religious beliefs in any society or ethnic or religious community deeply affect attitudes to death. For those who believe in "life after death" there is a feeling of continuance, community and celebration as seen in traditional Christian funeral ceremonies in the UK. For example, in Ireland a "wake" was traditionally held the night before the funeral, and on the day of the funeral the mourners were accompanied by a band in a procession to the graveside. Rosemary Powers (1993) shows how in the late 20th century many of the traditional rituals, symbols and functional behaviours surrounding death and burial still survive in Ireland compared to many other countries in Western Europe. In the Scottish Highlands, for example, the deceased was customarily buried with salt and earth sprinkled on their chest. The earth symbolised the fact that the body decays and becomes a part of the earth; the salt does not decay and was used to symbolise the soul. This custom has almost died out except where it has been revived in a post-modern setting.

Other changes have also taken place in recent years. Traditionally in the Highlands women went to the church service but did not go to the graveside; now they tend to do so. In contrast to this we can see a continuance of traditional customs and practices in immigrant communities that hark back to their past in their "home" country before the diasporas. Firth (1993), for example, describes Hindu and Sikh approaches to death in Asian communities in Britain. She shows how important it is for health-care professionals to understand the different religious, cultural and family patterns and distinctive attitudes to death and dying, including those related to reincarnation. "There are rituals which need to be done at the moment of death, which make it essential for at least family members to be present; failing to do this can have long term consequences." (1993; p. 26).

Ethnic minority communities in the UK often affect practices in the wider society. Aspects of their various cultural beliefs and customs relating to death and dying are sometimes incorporated into those of the dominant culture and the individual's post-modern choice patterns of what constitutes a "good" death and burial. However, ethnic minority communities in the UK are also changed when the younger members of these communities, looking to their future, wish to adopt British ways and integrate more with the local population. The strains from the various forces at play can result in disruption and conflict within the communities. They undergo strain in their attempts to maintain tradition while keeping up with the many demands of living and dying in a society that is not always in tune with their traditions. Occasionally tragedy can result, such as the honour killing of young women who do not comply with certain outmoded cultural traditions that tend to subjugate women.

In recent years, however, interest in death and the experience of dying has been revived, especially in certain sectors of UK society. Thus, we have been made aware of how death can occur at any time through the deaths of younger people and members of the gay community, often in their prime, through AIDS-related illnesses in the 1980s and 1990s. Younger people are also dying violently due to our "contemporary killing" culture of suicide or knife and gun crime. There are also still notable differences in mortality between men and women in Western societies; men are still more likely to commit suicide and homicide and to be killed in accidents and wars than women. This applies particularly to young men.

There is also increasing awareness of the importance of a "good" death at any age, whether at home or in a hospice, with family and friends around and where pain and suffering are kept to a minimum.

Related to "end-of-life care" are the longstanding debates aired on the media in the UK concerning euthanasia. This is the practice of ending life according to the tenet of a so-called "good" death that is dignified and as painless as possible. Of course, approaches to this issue vary widely according to the culture of the social group concerned as well as moral, religious, personal and professional viewpoints. In contrast to the UK, the practice of euthanasia, or assisted death, has become legal in certain countries such as Switzerland, The Netherlands and Belgium. It has also caused the phenomenon known somewhat macabrely as "death tourism", whereby people desiring euthanasia in a medical setting travel to these countries for treatment. In the UK it remains illegal and has led to some high-profile cases of people going abroad for the purposes of assisted suicide, such as that of the British doctor with an incurable degenerative condition whose death was assisted in Switzerland by drinking barbiturates.

For some people, euthanasia is unacceptable under any circumstances. It goes against the Hippocratic Oath taken by medical physicians covering their ethical practice. However, there are different types of euthanasia, each carrying varying levels of acceptability and controversy. Euthanasia may be voluntary or involuntary, the latter involving proxy consent where an individual is incapacitated. Arguments in support of voluntary euthanasia are the right to choice, individual autonomy and independence, quality of life, and the economic and opportunity costs of treating those who desire death rather than those who do not. Passive euthanasia is the withholding of treatment and/or providing medication to ease pain when it is known that death will occur as a result. Non-aggressive euthanasia involves withholding life support that would otherwise prolong life. Aggressive euthanasia is the provision of lethal substances; unsurprisingly it is the most controversial.

Cultural comparisons relating to the family, old age and dying

Cultural comparisons

It is generally agreed that attitudes of family members influence the experience of the dying person. When caring for the elderly or the dying in the family, different cultural practices are reflected in the care given, as well as the ways in which grief is expressed following the death of a family member. What is clear is that from infancy to old age, and even when facing death, the family preserves and passes on the culture it embodies, while at the same time it is itself affected by changes in the broader culture. In a rapidly changing society, the family has to adjust to these cultural changes, and this affects its approach to death and dying. These adjustments can be painful and traumatic at both the family and individual levels, and the stresses and strains in a culture are often mirrored by tensions in family life, which may become most apparent at the time of death and bereavement.

The cycle linking birth and death reflects an important tie between parents and their children in that the former care for the latter during their dependency period and, in most cultures, the latter return this care and respect in later life and on the death of the parents. In cultures such as certain traditional African societies, parents of large families are seen as especially fortunate and are held in great esteem, not only during life but after death for as long as they are remembered by their descendants. The old play another important role in the family and society as "keepers of culture". In traditional societies this involves passing on their knowledge of traditions. All societies assign status with ascribed rights and duties according to age. This, along with gender, is used in many societies as a major basis for social differentiation. In many non-Western societies within the lineage, age is associated with corresponding signs of respect and obedience. For example, in China, India and most African societies, people who achieve old age have greater authority and prestige than other age groups. In societies that value knowledge, which depends on memory and experience, the old are venerated as knowing more than the young. However, in modern societies with falling birth rates and an ageing population, the status of the elderly has altered. In these neo-modern societies, there is more emphasis on change, innovation and new ideas, with the speed of change putting a premium on flexibility and an emphasis on youth. This often makes the experience and knowledge of the older members of society seem obsolete to the young.

Death and burial in traditional societies: some African examples

Death in traditional societies

Sociologists as well as social anthropologists have been generally interested in describing rituals and symbols used in the "rites of passage" that mark the various stages of the life cycle and help to keep order in wider society. Death followed by ceremonies such as funerals mark the last stage of the life cycle, when the dead are buried. Historical and cross-cultural concerns about burial and treatment of the dead body have often centred on religious beliefs. Thus views on the treatment of the dying and the body after death in different cultures in different historical eras were often related to beliefs about life after death and the resurrection of the body in the after-life (such as mummification and the elaborate ceremonies and rituals accompanying entombment in ancient Egypt).

In traditional societies when a person dies, he or she leaves behind property, roles and status. In such societies it is necessary to deal with death and its consequences in ways that are as least disturbing as possible to those who remain. In many cultures the dead are imbued with new roles and status, perhaps as spirits and/or ancestors. To confer such status on the dead, funeral and burial rituals are necessary. These rituals often symbolise not only a break with the old and with death, but also a movement to the new in rebirth. An example of this is given by the Yoruba people of Nigeria who believe in reincarnation and that there is a limbo between dying and being reborn. The next birth in the lineage, of a child of the same sex as the deceased person, is quickly recognised as the person returning to the family. Names are given to the new child such as *babatunde* ("father has come back") or *Iyabo* ("mother has come back"), denoting the reincarnation of the loved one. However, the return of the dead is not always welcomed, particularly if the person who died was considered evil, because this would give rise to a malicious spirit. Among the Yoruba, attempts are made by parents of newborn *abiku* children to persuade them to avoid death once more and to stay alive and with them in the real world. *Abiku* are thought to be spirits who keep returning through birth only to die once more in order to return to the spirit world once again. In Ben Okri's (1991) Booker-prize winning novel *The Famished Road*, the narrator Azaro is an *abiku* or spirit child. The story follows him through his life, and his various encounters with the spirits who are constantly trying to return him to the spirit world. These beliefs may be linked to the high infant mortality rate in Southern Nigeria.

The aim of funeral rituals in these traditional societies is to make sure that the spirit of the dead person has a safe journey to the land of spirits or ghosts, even if this is only a temporary transition period before being reborn. An example of this is the way Yoruba people bury their dead beneath the veranda of the family home (although in recent times the use of public cemeteries and coffins has also increased in popularity). For similar reasons the Akan people of Ghana bury their dead in a clan burial ground. Food, drink and clothes may be buried with the corpse, much like the practices of the ancient Egyptians whereby such items would facilitate the journey to a new spiritual world. Among the chiefs and rulers (commonly referred to as *obas*) traditional customs involved the burial of slaves and even wives alongside the dead ruler. Historically the Oba of Benin was always accompanied to the after-life by members of his family and household.

Ceremonial feasts, or wakes, are usually held, especially if the person who died was old and highly respected. Their passing is marked by dancing, drumming and singing. The children of the dead person are responsible for seeing that they are buried according to proper ceremonial tradition and associated rituals. These are often so elaborate that debts may be incurred in order to pay for funeral expenses. This obligation may be shared by members of societies or groups to which the dead belonged. Among the Yoruba, the *Ogboni*, *Oro* and *Egungun* societies take an active part in the funerals of their members, as do the freemasons in Britain. Therefore, after the initial burial takes place, which may be reserved for close friends and kin, a second burial or ceremony also takes place. The extent to which such multiple markers are performed also relates to factors such as the societal status of the deceased and the readiness of the relations to pay for a second ceremony. This extension of rituals may relate to the former responsibilities of the deceased, which sometimes take time to unfold and reallocate

The dead body, death and dying

The dead body, death and dying

The treatment of the dead is a fascinating issue, closely bound up with cultural differences and attitudes to death, spirituality, religion and the human condition. Tradition and ritual are no less important after death has taken place than when one is preparing for the inevitable. Once dead, the treatment of dead bodies and human tissues, organs and skeletal remains by the living becomes germane. Thus some cultures and religions, such as Christian and Muslim faiths, believe in burial, while others, such as Hinduism, insist on cremation of their dead.

In many countries human organ donation is encouraged by the medical profession in order to help those in need of healthy organs for transplantation, such as hearts or livers. Donor cards have become commonplace and are carried by people wishing to donate their organs in the event of death. However, this is a very contentious issue as it intersects with key issues in religious, moral and cultural attitudes towards human body parts, death, the human soul and an after-life. Consent and respect lie at the heart of this highly complex issue. It causes significant problems for interested groups in health-care and related professions. Dominant cultural and moral attitudes, the wishes of the deceased person's family and the wishes of the dead person must all be taken into account.

High-profile examples of distress over the use of human organs after death include scandals at the Bristol Royal Infirmary and Alder Hey Children's Hospital, Liverpool, in the UK. In 1999 Alder Hey Hospital was found to have been responsible for the unautho-rised removal, storage and disposal of human tissue, including that of children, from the late 1980s until the mid-1990s. These were used for purposes such as medical research. A key piece of legislation arising as a result is the Human Tissue Act 2004, which came into force in September 2006 in England, Wales and Northern Ireland (The Human Tissue Scotland Act 2006 applies to Scotland). The legislation applies to the donation, removal, storage and use of human body parts. Interestingly, human tissue refers to "material other than gametes which consists of or includes human cells" (Human Tissue Authority, 2008). Blood is included in the definition, but hair and nails are not. An organisa-tion that was formally established in April 2005, the Human Tissue Authority, oversees the Act.

This legislation and the ethical, scientific and religious problems posed by these issues are by no means confined to the medical profession. Disciplines such as archaeology have had to grapple with complex debates in recent years about the balance between the need for scientific study or education and the cultural beliefs of source communities. These issues are perhaps no more acute than when human remains are involved. We are familiar with the sight of human remains in museums and other heritage sites, such as mummies from ancient Egypt. Beneath the city of Paris, in a network of caverns and tunnels that make up the Catacombs of Paris, there are countless bones and skulls of the city's dead. These crypts provide us with information about the past and form an important part of the city's history.

Many collections in museums in the Western world include human remains such as bones, skin, hair and teeth. The Pitt Rivers Museum in Oxford shows several shrunken heads, or *tsantsas*, as part of a display on "The treatment of dead enemies". They were acquired between 1871 and 1936 from the Upper Amazon region of South America between Peru and Ecuador (Pitt Rivers, 2008; Peers, 2003). However many source communities may be unhappy about the storage, analysis and display of the remains of their ancestors – there may be conflict with their beliefs about the treatment of the dead and the objectification of such human remains may cause them dismay. Requests have been made for repatriation of items like these for reburial or other religious ceremonies. This is a vivid illustration of how cultural attitudes towards death and dead bodies can vary markedly across societies, and reflects the tensions that still exist as a result of colonialism and the colonial mindset that dominated, especially during the 20th century, and with the advent of late modernity, when the importance of positivist science became a key force especially in the West. Different cultures hold different paradigmatic representations and value the dead in different ways. It is difficult to prioritise the needs or views of one group over another. Unfortunately, in this area compromise is very difficult – though not impossible – because of the passionate views of those who believe in science and those who believe in religious, cultural or other issues. It remains highly contested terrain. Of course, the age of some remains may mean that their provenance and origins are difficult to discern, or there may be no traceable living descendants.

Some museums are nevertheless obliged by legislation to consider the requests from source communities regarding the ethics of displaying human remains, such as respect for visitors as well as the dead, the manner of interpretation, the value of the display as opposed to other methods of communication. They should also seek advice from or consult with source communities and other relevant stakeholders wherever possible. Many large public museums and representative bodies like the Museum Ethnographers Group (1994) and the Department for Culture, Media and Sport (DCMS, 2005) now have explicit policies on human remains, and there are ethical codes that cover issues such as the display, interpretation and repatriation of sensitive material (Museums Association, 2002).

Cultural awareness and uses of the dead to the living

Cultural awareness

We have discussed the use of human remains by the living in terms of the donation of organs and other body parts for transplantation or research and for educational and scientific purposes, including preservation of bones and "shrunken" heads in museums and other heritage sites. We should also recognise that burial or cremation can also be viewed as a "use", in that the religious, practical, commemorative and other functions of such rituals and ceremonies play an important role for relatives and other members of society. This is an interesting point as "use" is a somewhat ambiguous term. From the perspective of positivist science, it may refer to practical and knowledge-based functions that seek to inform or enhance understanding and improve the quality of life for the living. From the perspective of religious, spiritual, cultural or other doctrines, it may be the act of remembrance. From the perspective of education or heritage, it may be increasing our understanding of the human body and how it works, or the past and other cultures.

One high-profile case in recent years that captured the public imagination and tapped into the problems surrounding use of human remains is that of anatomist Gunther von Hagens and his infamous *Body Worlds* exhibition. He invented a technique for preserving biological tissues called "plastination". His exhibition included numerous human cadavers plastinated, and often dissected, to allow viewers to observe the internal organs and other tissues. It commenced in 2005, exhibiting worldwide, and raising both public fascination and controversy. Some argue that it provides important insights and education for those interested in learning about the human body and physiology. Others are critical of the entertainment value of the exhibition and claim it is sensationalist and disrespectful of the dead. In the UK in November 2002 he carried out an autopsy live on television. This was followed by a series of television programmes featuring von Hagens called *Anatomy for Beginners* (2005), *Autopsy: Life and Death* (2006), and *Autopsy: Emergency Room* (2007).

Perhaps such ventures do increase knowledge and awareness of the human body and stimulate interest in medicine, anatomy and pathology; perhaps they are sensationalist, disrespectful and in bad taste. Either way, it is unlikely that the issue will be resolved in the next few years. Furthermore, controversy and debate are more likely to increase as techniques in medicine and science improve and threaten the values of more traditional or religious sentiments.

Other contested and controversial issues relating to the treatment and use of the dead include consent, dignity, methods of acquisition and disposal, partial use of cadavers and dissection, wilful donation before and/or after death by the individual or next of kin, cause of death, source culture of the deceased, possible benefactors and motives thereof, the timing of death (e.g. recent death or bones recovered during an archaeological dig) and the treatment of the vulnerable in society including prisoners undergoing execution, people who die while incarcerated, those who die in hospital, children and the elderly. This list is by no means exhaustive but it indicates the complexity surrounding any discussion of the uses of the dead by the living. While many uses are possible, we must be concerned about (arguably most importantly) justifying whatever use is made, and we must always respect the beliefs and attitudes of family members about the bodies of their loved ones.

Conclusions

This chapter has considered how death, dying and dead bodies are viewed and dealt with in different societies and cultures.

Perspectives on death and dying

Adopting a primarily sociological critique, these three interrelated concerns were woven into a discussion about the way in which societal, cultural and historical influences shape diverse attitudes, rituals, social and even legal structures. Death and dying can be viewed both as processes and as inevitable outcomes, or events, awareness of which weighs heavily on the minds of the living in most cultures and societies. Issues of ageing, illness, religion, tradition, kinship, ethnicity, science, medical care and morality thus become germane in our conceptions, experiences and depictions of death and dying, at both a societal and an individual level. Dead bodies, including human skeletal remains and tissue and organs, provide physical remnants of past lives which are of no less concern than the living. Living people who donate organs are unlikely to suffer loss of life as a result of this act, but ultimately it is the living who decide how to deal with the legacy of dead bodies and their tissues. This is even more complex when the wishes of the dead person are not known, or when conflicting viewpoints are held, or the passing of time makes the provenance of human remains difficult to discern.

The aim of our discussion was to map out, from a sociological standpoint, the important issues and tensions inherent in the treatment of death, dying and dead bodies. This subject raises important questions about the human condition. We will all be affected by death, regardless of our culture, religion or other distinguishing factors, and it is hoped that these issues will have stimulated your own thinking about death, dying and dead bodies in relation to your own culture, beliefs, values and norms.

Reflective questions

1. What important roles do ceremonies that mark the passing of an individual (burial, cremation, wakes, etc.) provide for kin, communities and societies as a whole?

2. How do people in traditional, modern and neo-modern societies view ageing and death?

3. How do you want your own body, and body parts, to be used after you are dead, and why?

4. What do you think will become key areas of concern and debate

in relation to death, dying and the dead body in 50 years time?

5. What do you think are the challenges for health-care professionals in caring for dying people and their families in a multicultural society?

References and further reading

Aries, P. (1981). *The Hour of Our Death*. London, Allen Lane.

Department for Culture, Media and Sport (2005). *Guidance for the Care of Human Remains in Museums*. London, DCMS.

Dickinson, D. and Johnson, M. and Katz,. J.S. (eds) (1993). *Death, Dying and Bereavement*. Milton Keynes, The Open University.

Durkheim, E. (1915). *The Elementary Forms of Religious Life: A Study in Religious Sociology*. London, Allen and Unwin.

Durkheim, E. (1952). *Suicide: A Study in Sociology*. London, Routledge and Kegan Paul. First published 1897.

Firth, S. (1993). Approaches to death in Hindu and Sikh communities in Britain. In: D. Dickinson and M. Johnson (eds) *Death, Dying and Bereavement*. Milton Keynes, The Open University.

Glaser, B. and Strauss, A. (1965). *Awareness of Dying*. Chicago, Aldine.

Gorer, G. (1965). *Death, Grief, and Mourning in Contemporary Britain*. London, Cresset.

Human Tissue Authority (2008). *Human Tissue Act 2004*. London, Office of Public Sector Information. Available at http,//www.opsi.gov.uk/acts/acts2004/ukpga_20040030_en_1 (last accessed February 2009).

Kubler-Ross, E. (1969). *On Death and Dying*. New York, Macmillan.

Museum Ethnographers Group (1994). Professional guidelines concerning the storage, display, interpretation and return of human remains in ethnographical collections in United Kingdom Museums. *Journal of Museum Ethnography*, 6, 22–24.

Museums Association (2002). *Code of Ethics for Museums, Ethical Principles for all who Work for or Govern Museums in the UK*. London, Museums Association.

Okri, B. (1991). *The Famished Road*. London, Jonathan Cape.

Peers, L. (2003). Strands which refuse to be braided: hair samples from Beatrice Blackwood's Ojibwe collection at the Pitt Rivers Museum. *Journal of Material Culture*, 8(1), 75–96.

Pitt Rivers Museum (2008) *Human remains in the Pitt Rivers Museum*. Available at http://www.prm.ox.ac.uk/human.html (last accessed February 2009).

Powers, R. (1993). Death in Ireland: Death, wakes and funerals in contemporary Irish society. In D. Dickinson and M. Johnson (eds) *Death, Dying and Bereavement*. Milton Keynes, The Open University, pp. 21–25.

Perspectives on death and dying

Seale, C. (1998). *Constructing Death. The Sociology of Dying and Bereavement.* Cambridge, Cambridge University Press.

Walter, T. (1994). *The Revival of Death.* London and New York, Routledge.

Walter, T. (1998). *On Bereavement, The Culture of Grief.* Buckingham, Open University Press.

Chapter 4
A dying language
James Moir

The two old, simple problems ever intertwined,
Close home, elusive, present, baffled, grappled.
By each successive age insoluble, pass'd on,
To ours to-day – and we pass on the same.

Life and Death by Walt Whitman (1819–1892)

Introduction

There has been considerable debate surrounding the issue of Western societies being inherently "death-denying" (Aries, 1974). Some have argued that this does not apply to more modern times, while others have argued that it has never applied (Kellehear, 1984; Walter, 1991; Seale, 1998). However, as Zimmerman (2007) notes, there has been little discussion of why this issue of "denial" has risen up the sociological league table of topical debate, particularly given its psychological connotations.

Whatever the case, it is clear that there are various discourses about death and dying, a "dying language", so to speak. The study of this discourse is important, given that it can lead to an understanding of the kinds of explanation people have available to place death within the context of their lives. This "dying language" is likely to share much with general everyday discourse, in terms of talk about people, thoughts, feelings, meanings, intentions, actions, circumstances and relationships. It should not therefore be viewed as necessarily being about denial of death, but rather should be opened up for scrutiny in order to explore how people make use of everyday language to talk about death.

Perspectives on death and dying

There is a real need to examine everyday conversation about death and also to examine how death is discussed by people in situations where it is imminent. At first glance, this academic approach may appear a somewhat detached and disrespectful way of treating people's experience of death. However, the point is not to treat such talk as "how they come to terms with or understand death", nor indeed is it about passing judgement on people's discourse as a form of denial or inability to face up to death. Rather, the analytic aim is to examine the way both sides of this discourse are oriented – when individuals talk about "denying death" or "facing up to death".

This necessarily involves an examination of the psychological language that people access, as well as notions of the underlying basis for people's actions. Essentially this comes down to looking at how people refer to what is and is not within their control in relation to death. This discourse also includes that used by social scientists when they refer to "a death-denying culture". This is often presented in opposition to the notion of "a good death", referring to a death that a person accepts and feels prepared for. However, even this is not straightforward, as there is also a range of discourses about sudden death, and indeed how this can be "a better death" in certain cases. And, to complicate matters further, as Potter and Wetherell (1987) point out, people apply language in sometimes contradictory ways in order to justify, rationalise, explain and excuse their own actions or the actions of others.

This chapter focuses on contradiction and flexibility in discourse, as well as the discursive "grammar" people use when talking about the issue of agency in the face of what is taken as being an inevitable outcome for us all. Agency is conventionally associated with how people think and feel, and the way their thoughts and feelings affect their actions. People die in many different ways, which in turn are talked about in different ways. Much of this talk centres on the question of how much influence people can exert over events before they die, in terms of making clear their intentions, motives and feelings for the benefit of those who will live on. These psychological representations allow for various ways of talking about dying and making death intelligible as a part of both institutional and private life.

The discourse of thoughts and feelings

References to "thinking", "giving reasons", "knowing", "interpreting" or "understanding" issues surrounding death provide a kind of grammar for engaging with others when dealing with death. Here I use the word grammar to refer to a set of normative rules that can be applied when referring to people's actions and their accountability. Take, for example, references to "thinking things through" in relation to "putting one's affairs in order" in the face of a terminal illness. This kind of discourse provides a yardstick for agency, with respect to various actions, such as making decisions about matters including treatment options and quality of life, or personal and financial arrangements for surviving relatives after death. Rational discourse of this sort is therefore something that people are expected to engage in when faced with death within a certain timeframe. It provides a means of ordering their lives in the face of death, laying down a basis for action and a way to consider, judge and assess the actions taken.

However, whereas there is a normative grammar of reason, which provides elements of rationality and control as a means of facing up to death, there is also an affective or emotional element, representing feelings, that can also be taken as an accountable basis for action in relation to death. The emotional basis for action can be presented as understandable, as a means of literally moving a person to do something or indeed to do nothing. It is often portrayed as an influence on how people think things through. Thinking is taken as being rational, as applying reason, whereas emotion is seen as providing a means of either supporting or skewing the reasoning process.

In relation to death, there is often a considerable range of emotion talk, as people express their feelings about what has happened or is about to happen. Much of this talk centres around either being in denial of death or facing up to death. This issue is commonly considered as an emotional process or response to death. Facing up to death is often viewed as being "healthy", even necessary, while other responses may be viewed as being "maladaptive" or even "pathological". Denial is taken as interfering with the process of acceptance of death and being "rational" about it. The dying person may be perceived as being in denial, or their surviving relatives and friends may be seen to react in this way. Emotion surrounding death can therefore be discursively constructed as an obstacle to dealing with death or as a positive means of coming to terms with it.

This duality is interesting in terms of the ways in which emotion discourse can be a flexible and useful means of characterising action. As Edwards (1997) notes, references to feelings can be put to a great variety of uses within a range of social practices due to the flexibility of emotions as ways of accounting for actions:

(i) They can be contrasted with cognitions in terms of their less deliberative and more spontaneous nature.

(ii) They can be taken as being 'understandable' and appropriate, as how any reasonable person would react.

(iii) They can be characterised as being the outcome of events or inherent in the nature of the person.

(iv) They can be treated as being kept under control through a person's reasoning or as reactions that resist control.

(v) They can be presented as the interaction of mental and physiological systems, as natural, or as derived from moral and ethical concerns.

I want to make a case for examining how this "grammar" for the structuring of a dying language is bound up with managing ways of dying. This framework overcomes some of the problems associated with attempts to describe Western societies in terms of whether they are, or are not, essentially death-denying. Studying how people talk about death in terms of a discursive psychology permits an analysis of the ways in which agency is managed with respect to those who have died or are dying, and those people who have survived or will survive the deceased. Death and dying are crucial in how we construct agency. Clearly, the "event" of dying changes what people are like "inside" as thinking and feeling agents.

The notion of an inner psychological architecture is the basis of much of our everyday discourse, which trades on the assumption that people want to interact in order to understand each other's thoughts and feelings. This is part of a wider cultural commonplace, the idea of an "inner/outer" dualism, which is integral to a range of social practices. The discursive construction of these two separate realms is therefore a major rhetorical feature in how people interact with one another, expressing notions of "sense making" as well as portraying people's "inner" mental states. There is a huge cultural imperative to be able to convey one's thoughts and feelings in the form of judgements, reasons and evaluations, as the outcome of a mental process. This everyday "grammar" is therefore central to the social practices that people engage in, including how they "deal" with death.

Essentially, people want to know the minds of others. This imperative provides a way of ordering how we talk to one another. We need to understand mental processes in order to account for how we perceive matters as a basis for action. In this way death is placed as an "event", as needing to be understood and talked about in terms of emotional response. In this communication model, there is an outer realm of people placed in amongst events and occurrences and an internal realm of mental operations, and these two realms need to be brought together. Here, "coming to terms with death" is associated with the psychological notion of "adjustment". Accounting for death is presented as a means by which people make sense of what has happened and come to terms with it. Death is therefore something that can be seen as confronting us, in terms of how we display ourselves, or in terms of how we understand others who are confronted by it, as psychological agents in the world. We account for death in some way or other: as natural, inevitable, tragic, accidental, or we may even refer to it as "making no sense". It is interesting to note that each of these accounts will be bound up with a range of emotional discursive constructions as the basis for the accountability or the intelligibility of reactions to death. We can "understand" why a person might react in a particular way, given certain circumstances surrounding a particular death.

Death as "open" or "withheld" communication

Talking and not talking

As noted above, death is something that needs to be talked about, even bearing in mind the notion that one of the reactions to death is not to talk about it. Talking about death is sometimes regarded as beneficial and therapeutic and this perception is commonly associated with aspects of care related to death such as palliative care and bereavement counselling. This belief is based on an assumption about discourse; namely, that talking is in itself helpful, and that talking about death is necessary in order to face up to it and deal with it. Not talking about death is associated with the psychological notion of denial, often taken as a sign of a (normative) temporary state that will give way to an "opening up" and a confronting of death. This kind of discourse about "denial" is a common construction that is often used as a means of persuasion of the need for change. The notion here is of a "defence mechanism" that is somehow a "natural" part of the psychological process, which may or may not require "facilitation" to help the person come to terms with death.

On the other hand, there is also a discourse about death that involves protecting a dying person from knowing about their true medical condition due to concern about how this news would be taken. This notion of withholding communication may feature as part of a discussion with relatives about the vulnerability of the dying person. However, an aspect of this discourse centres on the ethical issues associated with this stance. Some people may take the view that such withholding of communication is dishonest, no matter what the circumstances. However, for others, the argument may be one of "what is in the best interests of the dying person". Here, agency is vested in others by way of them "knowing" the person's true vulnerability, or in the desire to ensure that the person can stay hopeful and optimistic during their remaining time. This can lead to concerns about whether this counts as lying or omission of the full medical facts. A reluctance to acknowledge or reveal a terminal prognosis can therefore provoke discussions amongst relatives and medical practitioners about the agency of the person who is dying and what they have the right to know.

Death and institutional discourse

Institutional discourse

For some people, the institutional nature of death, whether in a hospital or hospice, is a particularly pressing issue. This discourse again cuts both ways. For some, the argument centres around whether or not the dying person should be removed from their home and everyday relationships. Here the argument is that death should not be institutionalised but rather that a dying person should be able, as far as possible, to be at home and interact with relatives. However, for others, it is the medical care available that is of paramount importance, especially the availability of effective pain relief. It is interesting to note how this discourse mirrors that surrounding birth, where the issue of home versus hospital births has been a topic of debate on and off over the past few decades.

However, views on this "home or institution" issue may change in the person who is dying as well as their relatives as time proceeds or an illness progresses. This raises the point that people can "change their minds" and that death can involve "decisions" and "choices". Again, we come back to the issue of the agency of the individual and the notion of a "managed death". The dying person and their family are expected at certain points in the course of a terminal disease to accept and prepare for death in a responsible fashion, and to take decisions along the way about the level of institutional support they require at particular junctures. They must therefore enter into a discourse with members of the medical institution about the course of an illness and what this may entail. This in turn sets up further complications involving the difficulties of understanding medical terminology, and the power of some medics to drive such decisions in terms of "advice" offered, and about the extent to which issues are even framed as decisions at all. For example, patients and relatives may be presented with medical records and documentation that are taken as providing an irrefutable rationale for a particular course of action. It could be argued that it is difficult to disagree in the face of such evidence and that those who attempt to do so may be characterised by medics as being "noncompliant" or "in denial". Such characterisations can therefore be used by medical professionals as ways of countering resistance to the dominant notions of the "correct" way to behave in the face of a terminal illness.

However, this is not simply a one-way street. Those medics who persist with treatments that are ineffective, and can end up being counter-productive for the dying person's dignity, may also be accused of being "in denial". In this context, denial is perhaps most closely related to the argument of Aries (1974) about the death-denying nature of Western society and is often used to support the case for voluntary euthanasia. This argument is based on the idea that those who are dying have a right to a particular "quality of life" as expressed through the notions of human rights and human dignity. There is also the criticism that the use of sophisticated technology to maintain life when someone is dying is undignified and wasteful of limited healthcare resources. Sometimes implicit in this argument is the view that medics can be egotistical in their zeal to prolong life and that their sense of agency, in "fighting" ill-health and death, is sometimes counter-productive.

Beyond the psychologisation of death denial

Death denial

My concern in this chapter is not with whether we are in reality death-denying or death-accepting on a social or individual level. Rather, I am interested in the usage of "denial" as a way of experiencing or perceiving death. Focusing on the discourse of death offers an opportunity to examine how agency works in relation to death. The concept of a mental system that operates upon an external reality in order to produce a perception of that reality effectively separates cognitive activity from social practice. This dualistic discourse strips out what I have tried to highlight above, namely that death and dying throw up all manner of notions about the "right way" or "wrong way" to die and to "face up to death". These discourses involve many different characterisations of agency, interests and relationships that rest upon certain underpinning moral, political, religious and economic foundations. They are not merely about "how people perceive matters"; they actually play a part in creating those perceptions.

A psychological account of "denial" as blocking proper and accurate perception is very much part-and-parcel of the lexicon of modern psychology, but it can also be found in less explicit ways within other, more unlikely, realms, which give more theoretical weight to social practice. As Potter and Edwards (2001) point out, the social theorist Pierre Bourdieu may be considered an unlikely advocate of a psychological account of human action but his theory of habitus (e.g. Bourdieu, 1977; 1992) is based on the concept of an unreflexive construction of mind. This presupposes the development of a psychological system in which dispositions associated with membership of social and cultural groups come to generate practices, perceptions and attitudes. This system is then able to produce "meaning" (i.e. make sense), store and process it. While Bourdieu gives more weight to social practice and culture than psychology, he cannot rid himself of this reification of "mind" as a perceptual system.

Academic disciplines such as psychology and sociology trade on this kind of discourse but it is also constructed and maintained in less formal academic ways, as part and parcel of everyday social practices, including that of talk about death and dying. An analytic stance that moves away from considering death denial as an underlying psychological issue and instead focuses on how we construct a "dying language" opens up the possibility of an approach that is much more connected to the world of social action and social order. When exploring this issue, it is unhelpful to start from the assumption that there is a psychological system that operates upon "events" in order to produce "thought" and "feelings". For one thing, such an assumption is not necessarily a cultural universal, and for another people themselves do not necessarily make reference to things "making sense" as they engage in various social practices. This is not to say that the phenomenon does not exist but rather that, for the purpose of studying "how people talk about death", we need not start from a position of trying to examine "how people perceive death". This stance immediately opens the way to examining how psychological discourse or implicit references to an underlying psychology are pressed into service in order to assert what is the "right" or "wrong" way to die.

It should also be noted that the position I advocate does not require any particular model of the individual or society. In other words, the focus is squarely upon the business of what gets constructed as how people deal with death and how this is accomplished as an aspect of social practice. By taking seriously the issue of a dying language in terms of what gets constructed – how, where and when – the more traditional approach to society and its actors as causal entities is bypassed altogether. By refraining from starting with some pre-defined model of the social actor, especially the traditional psychological model in which the problem becomes one of understanding "how people perceive matters", it becomes possible to treat talk about death and dying simply as a range of discourses that are maintained or challenged within a range of social practices.

This may all seem a bit abstract but the significance of such an analytical move is that it allows the focus of study to become the actual construction of a dying language. For most people, this is a matter of practical sociological construction as they make decisions, discuss relationships and generally engage in the living world that must deal with death. Much has been written recently about discursive psychology (e.g. Edwards and Potter, 1992; Edwards, 1997; Potter ,1996, Potter, 2003; te Molder and Potter, 2005) but there is much less discussion of how psychological agents are constructed in relation to the life course, and in particular death. As argued above, this can be considered as a grammar in terms of the ways in which matters are presented as needing to be made sense of, or in stressing the "inner" psychological processes.

Coming to terms with the language of death

The language of death

Let us therefore consider the means by which death is presented as an "event" and an aspect of the life course that confronts us and triggers a psychological response. This process involves constituting death in a particular way, not only as the moment when life ceases, but also as a state leading to an enduring social existence within surviving people's memories and reminiscences. Death is therefore talked about as an event that will normatively lead to these psychological phenomena. They will impinge upon the agency of the living in a way that is represented as enduring over time and is often associated with emotion. And as we have seen, in the case of those confronting terminal illness, death impinges upon both the dying person and the family in terms of the decisions that need to be made. In this way death is presented as something that evokes a psychological reaction and also as something that requires psychological effort in order to deal with it.

In a world where communication is considered a good thing in itself, expressing thoughts and feelings about those close to us who have died, or those who are terminally ill, is seen as being generally positive. We have seen how this "opening up" is treated as being honest and therapeutic. Therefore evidence of psychological labour, of thinking over matters, is taken as leading to a better understanding. However, as I have also pointed out, the issue arises of whether people are expending too much or too little psychological effort in confronting death. For example, to talk about the deceased "too much" is taken as being psychologically unhealthy and evidence of an inability to "move on with one's life". In this way talk about death becomes a vehicle for social judgement, as a reading of how well someone is dealing with it. Language also provides a means of dealing with expectations about the temporal nature of grief as a psychological process. There is a huge cultural imperative upon people to produce, or at least attempt to produce, normatively appropriate psychological discourse that fits with commonly accepted social relations and interactions. Again, those who are seen as breaching these expectations are perceived as "not coping" or "not coming to terms with death".

The idea of an "inner" psychological reaction to death is therefore a pervasive discursive cultural commonplace. This is a language of and about death that is taken as indicative of psychological reactions to it. Of course there is also another discourse, in which the way people talk is treated as "hiding" their "true" reaction, as being a discursive front. For example, if someone appears too upbeat, this may be taken as a sign of "putting on a brave face" in order to avoid public displays of emotional pain. As we have seen, the same discourse can therefore be "read" one way or another and interpreted as expressing different reactions to death.

Conclusion

What can be concluded is that there is a "dying language" in Western societies that is firmly rooted in treating people as psychological agents. There are also competing discourses on the right way to die and how to react to death. For example, some have argued that there is now a postmodern approach to grief, in terms of accepting that it is a matter of individual reaction, that the display of emotion is something that "works" for some and not others, and that forgetting is best for some and remembering is best for others (Hunt, 2005). Death therefore brings about a series of discursive dilemmas, requiring a language that describes how we confront it and react to it.

There have been sociological debates revolving around whether or not Western societies are death-denying, and many of these have involved batting back and forth positions on the institutionalisation and medicalisation of death and dying. Other debates have centred on the nature of self and the notion that people are increasingly being confronted with decisions about planning their own lives as well as their deaths. It is true that we now live in an era of personal development planning not just for our careers but also perhaps in terms of confronting and preparing for our own mortality. However, as I have shown, the extent of the individual's participation and agency in this process again varies greatly according to their particular circumstances.

In this chapter I have tried to show that, rather than getting bogged down in arguments for or against the death-denying nature of Anglo-American society, it is more analytically fruitful to consider how the concept of denial is treated as an explanatory resource that people draw upon when discussing death. This can be treated as a problem or an obstacle to "the right way to die", or it can be presented as beneficial, as a healthy reaction to death. It is not simply the case that it is always taken as being one or the other, but rather is very much bound up with assertions about death and dying. This approach is largely located within a discourse that centres on the notion of a psychological individual, who brings his or her mental realm to bear on confronting death as a basis for accountable action.

Also of interest is the categorisation of those who are dying and who are therefore being expected to confront death along with their families. In previous centuries people used to have much shorter periods of illness prior to death but modern medicine is able to diagnose terminal diseases earlier as well as extend people's lives. These medical advances not only have implications for the provision of institutionalised and home care of the "dying" but also the discourses that people engage in about agency with respect to the management of death. As Zimmerman (2007: 309) puts it:

> 'The necessity in modern medical care of the transfer of patients from acute care wards to palliative units and hospices (which necessitate the acknowledgement of a short prognosis), the discontinuation of nutrition and hydration, the signing of "do-not resuscitate" orders and completion of advance directives all result in a concomitant imperative to acknowledge and speak about dying.'

It is therefore arguably the case that in contemporary Western society there is a much greater focus on the management of the dying process than perhaps hitherto. This in turn is linked to the discussion of more issues surrounding death and dying, including that of death denial. The latter is therefore not somehow preventative of dealing openly with death but rather a reflexive and rhetorical construction associated with talk about what is the right way to die or deal with death. It is this discursive psychology related to the language of dying that needs to be opened up to scrutiny, for it is only by doing so that we can begin to come to grips with the way we talk about death and dying.

References and further reading

Aries, P. (1974). *Western Attitudes toward Death, from the Middle Ages to the Present*. Baltimore, Johns Hopkins University Press.

Bourdieu, P. (1977). *Outline of a Theory of Practice*. Cambridge, Cambridge University Press.

Bourdieu, P. (1992). *Language and Symbolic Power*. Cambridge, Polity Press.

Edwards, D. (1997). *Discourse and Cognition*. London, Sage.

Edwards, D. and Potter, J. (1992). *Discursive Psychology*. London, Sage.

Hunt, S. (2005). *The Life Course: A Sociological Introduction*. Basingstoke, Palgrave.

Kellehear, A. (1984). Are we a death-denying society? A sociological review. *Social Science and Medicine*, 18(9), 713–23.

Potter, J. (1996). *Representing Reality, Discourse Rhetoric and Social Construction*. London, Sage.

Potter, J. (2003). Discursive psychology: between method and paradigm. *Discourse and Society*, 14, 6, 783–94.

Potter, J. and Edwards, D. (2001). Sociolinguistics, Cognitivism and Discursive Psychology. In N. Coupland, S. Sarangi and C.N. Candlin (eds.) *Sociolinguistics and Social Theory*. Harlow, Essex, Pearson Education.

Perspectives on death and dying

Seale, C. (1998). *Constructing Death, The Sociology of Dying and Bereavement.* Cambridge, Cambridge University Press.

te Molder. H. and Potter, J. (eds.) (2005). *Conversation and Cognition.* Cambridge, Cambridge University Press.

Walter, T. (1991). Modern death, taboo or not taboo? *Sociology*, 25, 2, 293–310.

Zimmerman, C. (2007). Death denial, obstacle or instrument for palliative care? An analysis of clinical literature. *Sociology of Health and Illness*, 29, 2, 297–314.

Chapter 5
Death, social change and lifestyle in the UK
June L. Leishman

Do not go gentle into that good night
Old age should burn and rave at close of day;
Rage, rage against the dying of the light.

From *Do Not Go Gentle Into That Good Night* by Dylan Thomas (1914–1953)

Introduction

As identified earlier in this book, death is receiving a renaissance in attention in our society. After many years of silence it has again become a topic of public discussion. There are courses, seminars and conferences on death and dying; degrees in thanatology (the scientific study of death) are widely offered by universities and colleges across the UK, USA and other countries. In studying death and dying we are in essence exploring society's attitudes towards life and living, as well as gaining insights into cultures, rituals and customs. In some ways we have gone full circle in this area – early societies accepted death as a natural progression of life, one which was met with acceptance at a public and a personal level. In earlier centuries, when medicine and technology was not as advanced as it is today, death was a social norm that families experienced on a regular and recurring basis. Life expectancy was much lower, infant mortality was far greater, and death in childbirth was common. It was not unusual for children, family and close friends to be at the bedside of dying relatives, often together with someone from the clergy and a doctor. Indeed, early pictures of deathbed scenes clearly illustrate the public nature of dying as it was then.

Dying, death and bereavement (which many of us now only encounter at a personal level late in our lives with the death of a parent) are human events. They are embedded in numerous moral traditions and well-circumscribed by prescription for proper conduct that can be traced back to pre-modernity in religious terms, in which death was viewed as a transition from one existence or state to another, and calling on techniques of ritual engagement. Cultures can be death-denying, death-accepting, and even death-defying. As described by Philippe Aries (1981), the European experience of death has undergone significant transformations. Dying is not simply a basic feature of the human condition and the end of an individual's history. For many, but recognisably not all, there is also an element of individual agency in the lifestyle choices we make and how these affect and contribute to how well and how long we live. It is this element of individualism that is central to the focus of this chapter, which will explore individual lifestyle choices and the influence of science on the study of death and dying.

Social networks and the rise of individualism

Social networks and individualism

Social networks and kinships have always been a central feature of societies. These networks are socially constructed and take the form of family, extended family or small social groupings. One of the greatest changes in this area over time has been in family structures, the shift from extended to nuclear family units as viewed by Parsons (1951), the shift towards domesticity in the 18th century (Laine, 1996) and the growth of "affective individualism" (Stone, 1977) whereby people began to treat each other as unique individuals with personal and emotional needs. Four key social trends evolved during the 20th century. Community has been replaced by a pervasive sense of individualism; a predominantly religious world view has been taken over by one that is secular, with a rise in materialism and its power over values, and behaviours in the modern world and the influence of science and technology in our daily lives.

As social networks and kinships are social constructions, so too is death and dying. Death as a social construction means that it is defined using words, concepts, and ways of thinking available in the individual's culture (Kastenbaum, 1998). Because this meaning is socially constructed, death can mean different things to different people, and the meaning can change over time for each person. For some people, death is the end of their existence; for others, it is merely a point of transition to some higher spiritual life; and for yet others, it may mark the point at which the soul is released for rebirth into another body. Thus physical death is the end stage of a social process and it can be understood in the same way as other forms of social behaviours (Fulcher and Scott, 2007; p. 299). Chattoo *et al.* (2002) reminds us that kinship groups provide material, emotional and spiritual support and care during life-cycle events. Many families saw it as their responsibility to care for their dying relatives, and end-of-life care frequently occurred in the home. However with changing family structures, this is now less common.

Family life has also changed significantly over time. We no longer have the nuclear family or social networks that were the source of support during illness and death. It is also now uncommon in our society for people to die at home. We have sequestered dying to hospitals, care homes and hospices. Modern technology, such as life-support machines, oxygen delivery systems, resuscitators and sophisticated pain-control systems, form the landscape of modern medical institutions. Dying and death in many households now lies in the domain of the medical profession. Historically there were few options of a place for someone to end their life. Dying relatives were cared for at home, and the experience of dying parents, siblings and grandparents would have been common at a much earlier age.

Death and dying in the UK

Death and dying in the UK

There is no getting away from the fact that death happens. It is also true that as a society we do not encounter dying people in the ways our predecessors did. And when we do, it is generally at a later stage in our lives than our ancestors. Two social factors play a significant part in this in the UK: namely, the lowering of infant mortality rates and the increase in adult life expectancy (see Fig. 5.1).

Perspectives on death and dying

Rate per million population

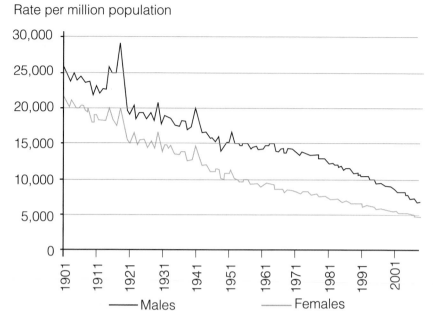

Figure 5.1 **Infant mortality rates**

Over the course of the 20th century there were fairly steady falls in these rates, although during the first half of the century the year-on-year fluctuations were particularly noticeable, mainly because of influenza epidemics and some unusually cold winters. The death rate for males fell from 25,829 per million in 1901, to 8,477 in 2000. The rate for females fell from 21,705 to 5,679 per million over the same period. And these trends have continued in the 21st century. Between 2001 and 2007 the death rate for males fell by 15 per cent, from 8,230 to 6,957 deaths per million, while for females it decreased by 11 per cent, from 5,566 to 4,926 per million.

The second social factor that impacts on our encounters with dying people is the medicalisation of death. In the 21st century in the UK, life expectancy is much greater as a result of improved lifestyles and modern medicine and medical technology. Alongside this, infant mortality is significantly lower. It is also very uncommon for women to die during childbirth. In every age and in every society, use has been made of whatever technological resources are available. Western medicine is unique with respect to the increasingly important role – practical and symbolic – played by technology in both diagnosis and treatment. Medical technologies, as complex systems, are more than physical objects used for particular purposes. They are cultural products that tell us something about the social, economic and historical values that produce them at a particular time and place. The increasing use of life-support systems, dialysis machines, monitoring equipment and incubators, as well as the new reproductive technologies, contribute to the blurring of the boundary between self and non-self. Kirmayer (1992) describes the experience of a haemodialysis patient who witnesses his own blood leaving his body, and travelling through plastic tubing into the dialysis machine before being returned to his own body. In the care of the dying, life-support machines can extend the period between biological death and social death. In this supported state, the body can exist for weeks or months, even years.

Health and lifestyle in the UK

Health and lifestyle in UK

Changes in attitudes, behaviours and lifestyle impact on our lives, as we live them, right up to the point of death. The medical and health-care professions have evolved and developed over time. Contemporary specialist professional roles are a result of the changing needs of society as they relate to health and heath trends and individual lifestyle choices.

Across all four nations of the UK, health and lifestyle issues share common ground in terms of health priorities, commitment to health-promotion strategies and awareness of other factors that influence the nation's health. Based on data from the World Health Organization (WHO, 1997), premature deaths will result from cardiovascular disease, diabetes, lung disease and certain cancers. This is twice as many deaths as from all infectious diseases combined. The WHO believes that prevention of disability and death from chronic non-communicable diseases (CNCDs) is not receiving sufficient attention, and they identify smoking, sedentary lifestyle and obesity as the top culprits (although longer lifespan also plays a role in some of the diseases).

However, any discourse related to health concerns and morbidity must also include issues such as housing conditions, educational attainment, employment and financial factors. These wider determinants of health are essential for promoting better health in the long term. If the UK is truly to become "a healthier nation", action in all these areas is needed. In a speech to the National Health Service in January 2008, the British Prime Minister, Gordon Brown, outlined a programme of "deeper and wider" reform of the NHS to help it face the challenges of the 21st century. He listed a number of measures for improving health prospects, including new screening procedures for a range of conditions such as heart disease, colon cancer, breast cancer, stroke and kidney disease. He stated that such conditions affect the lives of more than six million people, cause 200,000 deaths each year and account for a fifth of all hospital admissions (www.PM.gov.uk).

The general picture presented by the *Health Profile of England* survey (2007) was of an overall improvement in the health outcomes of a range of critical areas – the declining mortality rates in cancer, circulatory diseases and suicide – coupled with an increased life expectancy (the highest ever). However, the statistics for England also reveal that there are still some challenging problems, namely obesity and diabetes in adults and children, cigarette smoking, and drinking among young people. The report also identified a number of inequalities across geographical areas (Department of Health, 2007). Scotland's overall health profile continually lags behind that of England; in 1991 the standardised mortality rates were 12 per cent higher than those in England. Until recently, this seemed to depend almost entirely on the relatively lower levels of affluence in Scotland. Carstairs and Morris (1991) found that differences in levels of deprivation explained all but 3 per cent of the higher mortality rates in Scotland in 1981. However, Hanlon and his colleagues (2005) showed that by 1991 deprivation explained only 40 per cent of the excess deaths in Scotland.

The Welsh Assembly Government consultation document entitled *Well-Being in Wales* emphasised that the health of the nation is not the responsibility of the Welsh Assembly or the National Health Service alone. It stresses that everyone has a part to play to help improve health in Wales. This notion of shared responsibility between organisations and individuals was reinforced by the *Review of Health and Social Care in Wales 2004* (the Wanless Report), which stresses that trends in demand for health and care services are unsustainable in the longer term. The Welsh approach places greater emphasis on preventing ill health in the first place. This is essential if Wales is to shake off traditionally high levels of poor health still evident in many Welsh communities. In 2006 a review of public health organisations in Wales recommended that

> "A unifying public health strategy for Wales should be developed. This will shape long-term objectives for organisations and units delivering the public health function, and enable a performance framework to be developed to measure progress against public health issues".

In October 2006, Welsh Assembly ministers called for a strategic framework for public health to be developed. A project has been set up within the Public Health and Health Professions Department to support the development of a public health strategic framework. In November 2007, Health Minister Edwina Hart agreed seven themes for the strategic framework, and these are now being taken forward by Task and Finish Groups. These themes are:

- socioeconomic, cultural and environmental conditions
- children and young people
- healthy eating, food and fitness
- health-related behaviours and risk
- limiting long-term health conditions
- mental health
- strengthening local public health delivery.

In Northern Ireland, the Irish Health Minister Michael McGimpsey emphasised that upholding a healthy lifestyle must be a priority for all. The Minister was speaking at the Balmoral Show, while attending a promotional event by the Department of Health, Social Services and Public Safety and the Health Promotion Agency, where visitors are given advice on how simple lifestyle changes can have a positive impact on their level of health. During his visit, Mr McGimpsey said:

> "It is clear from recent reports that obesity levels in Northern Ireland are growing. One in four girls, one in five boys, and over half our adult population are now overweight

or obese. This is clearly a worrying trend that can ultimately result in serious medical conditions such as heart disease and diabetes and a generation full of problems for our young children. It is the responsibility of us all to ensure that our own personal health is a top priority. Small lifestyle changes can lead to huge benefits. A balanced diet and a more active lifestyle is the key. People are often put off when the words vegetables and exercise are used but it is about making small, sustained, long-term changes. Take a walk to the shops rather than [using] the car, substitute full-fat milk with semi-skimmed milk, and gradually introduce more fruit, vegetables and physical activity into your daily routine."

The Minister concluded:

"I understand that in this fast moving world of today, it can often be thought difficult to find the time for upholding a healthy lifestyle. Personal health is, however, too important to put on the back burner. Small dietary changes and more physical activity could potentially increase life expectancy and lead to a greater quality of life."

Issues identified across the UK are reflected in media and press coverage. Media headlines, such as those in Table 5.1 below, suggest that the UK *does* have a health crisis. If it is not addressed, it will result in chronic health conditions and death for many people.

Table 5.1 **Headline health stories from the British media in 2008**

From *The Independent* (15 July 2008):
HEALTH CHIEF SUPPORTS TOTAL DRINK BAN ON YOUNG DRIVERS

This article described ongoing discussions about imposing a no-alcohol rule among drivers aged 17 to 20 in the UK. The rationale was that young people are more affected by small amounts of alcohol than older people and are also less conscious of the risks, so they are more likely to drive after drinking. Their relative inexperience of driving, plus their alcohol intake, results in more crashes and therefore more deaths. Countries that already have a lower limit for young drivers – or a zero tolerance policy – report dramatic reductions in crashes involving young drivers. Further comments were made about other health risks among this age group, including violence, lack of exercise, unhealthy diets, risky sex, smoking, binge-drinking and drug-taking.

Death, social change and lifestyle in the UK

From *The Scotsman* (26 January 2008):

SCOTS ALCOHOL DEATH RATE TWICE THAT OF UK

Basing its discussion on figures taken from the Office for National Statistics for 2006, this article discussed the rising numbers of alcohol-related deaths in Scotland – more than twice as many deaths in Scotland as in the whole of the UK. There were more than 10,000 alcohol-related deaths throughout the UK, yet another increase from the previous year. Two-thirds of them were men, and the biggest increase was seen in men aged between 35 and 54. This trend among younger men was put down to the fact that most of them had been drinking heavily for most of their lives.

From *Telegraph Online* (26 February 2008):

BRITAIN NEAR TOP OF HEART DEATH LIST

A study published in the *European Heart Journal* revealed that people aged 45 to 74 in England and Wales are more likely to die from heart disease than French people, as well as Scottish people and residents of deprived Eastern European countries like Slovenia and Albania (but less likely to die than people in Ireland). The French population officially had the healthiest hearts in Europe, and this continues to be related to their good diet comprising red wine, olive oil, fruit and vegetables. However, others commented that the situation in France is merely a legacy of their lifestyle 30 or 40 years ago, when French people consumed lower-fat diets, had lower cholesterol levels and smoked and drank less than they do today.

From *Mail Online* (7 August 2008):

INSIDE THE FIRST NHS FAT CAMP FOR CHILDREN

Obesity costs the NHS around £1 billion a year directly and the UK economy over £2 billion a year. It has been predicted that around two-thirds of British children will be overweight or obese by 2050 and 4.5 million may die young unless they tackle their excess weight. This article described a possible long-term solution to the problem. One primary care trust in Yorkshire, an area much criticised previously by the media for its poor eating habits, began funding some 2000 clinically obese children to attend the first NHS-sponsored weight management camp. A third of the children in this area are already obese. The first stage of the programme is a summer camp where the emphasis is on a balanced healthy diet and adequate exercise. The children then attend a 24-week follow-up programme, together with their parents, in order to maintain their healthier lifestyle. The article also states how ironic this development is, given that in the same week the Government announced that the word 'obese' should be banned for referring to children with weight problems. Several children gave their opinions about these camps, together with stories about the bullying and name-calling they endure, and their hopes for a brighter future.

These headlines reveal that there are concerns for the health of the population of all the UK nations, and if we do not all attend to these concerns the life expectancy of a great many people in the

UK will be seriously compromised. The notion that individuals are responsible for their own demise is a challenging concept. However, moving on from the lifestyle choices that influence health, illness and ultimately death, there are also other "ways" of dying that form an integral part of the death and dying debate. These issues will be addressed later in this book.

Conclusions

Our responses to any situation in our lives are a direct result of our beliefs concerning that situation. Individual and societal beliefs about what dying is and what happens after death create many of the feelings that arise when we are faced with a life-threatening illness or with losing a loved one. In some cultures, or groups within a culture, there is an attempt to integrate the fact of mortality into the centre of living so that members are actively encouraged to see death as normal and to face the fact that each of us will die. In others, there is a tendency to combat or deny the fact of death, to the extent that life becomes an exercise in keeping thoughts of death at bay. This has been seen in our society as it has moved from a pre-modern to a modern society. Yet it is true that some ways of life and systems of belief do actively prepare people to acknowledge the reality of death, while others encourage denial of that reality. Mostly we find ourselves somewhere between the two, shifting back and forth according to the situation, time, place, company or age and so on. It is almost as though denial and affirmation of death form two ends of a continuum along which we move. Despite being a more informed society and having access to scientific data related to health and lifestyle, we are a society of people for whom health concerns that compromise health and advance early death remain significantly problematic. This is especially so in the United Kingdom.

This chapter has introduced several issues that impact negatively on the health of this country in the 21st century. The chapters that follow will develop the death and dying debates further.

Death, social change and lifestyle in the UK

Reflective questions

1. Write down five key things that you think affect life expectancy and identify what you do to stay healthy?

2. Compare the major causes of death in the early 1900s with the major causes today and consider what has led to these differences?

3. What has changed in the structure of society that influences our thinking about death and dying?

4. Think about your own social network. Using the circle below, map your family and friends in terms of their closeness to you, placing yourself in the middle.

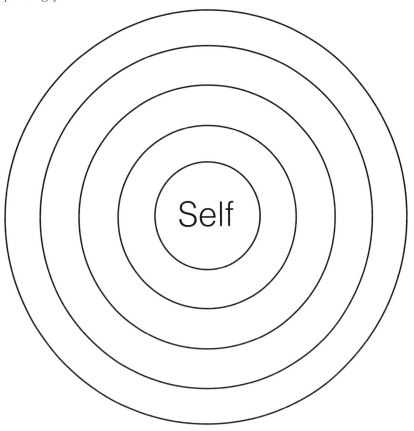

Self

5. What does your map tell you about your social network?

References and further reading

Aries, P. (1976). *Western Attitudes Towards Death*. London, Marion Boyars.

Aries, P. (1981). *The Hour of Our Death*. New York, Knopf.

Carstairs, V. and Morris, R. (1991). *Deprivation and Health in Scotland*. Aberdeen, Aberdeen University Press.

Cartwright, A., Hockey, L. and Anderson, J. (1973). *Life before Death*. London, Routledge.

Chattoo, S., Ahmand, W., Haworth, M. and Lennard, R. (2002). *South Asian and White patients with advanced cancer. Patients' and families' experiences of the illness and perceived needs for care. Final Report to CRC UK and the Department of Health*. Leeds, University of Leeds.

Cobb, M. (2002). *Facing Death, The Dying Soul*. Buckingham, Open University Press.

Department of Health (2007). *Health Profile of England Survey*. Available at: http://www.dh.gov.uk/en/Publicationsandstatistics/Publications/PublicationsStatistics/DH_079716 (last accessed Febuary 2009).

Dinnage, R. (1990). *The Ruffian on the Stair, Reflections on Death*, London, Viking.

Fenwick, P. and Fenwick, E. (1996). The near-death experience. In: P. Badham and P. Ballard (eds). *Facing Death*. Cardiff, University of Wales Press.

Fulcher, J, and Scott, J. (2007). *Sociology*, 3rd edn. Oxford, Oxford University Press.

General Register Office for Scotland (2007). *Registrar General Reports on Deaths Last Winter*.
Available at: http://www.gro-scotland.gov.uk/press/2007-news/registrar-general-reports-on-deaths-last-winter.html (last accessed February 2009).

Giddens, A. (2006). *Sociology*, 4th edn. Cambridge, Polity Press.

Glaser, B.G. and Strauss, A.L. (1967). *The Discovery of Grounded Theory*. New York, Aldine.

Grey, M. (1985). *Return from Death*. London, Arkana.

Hanlon, P., Lauder, R.S., Buchanan, D., *et al.* (2005). Why is mortality higher in Scotland than in England and Wales? Decreasing influence of socioeconomic deprivation between 1981 and 2001 supports the existence of a "Scottish Effect". *Journal of Public Health*, 27(2),199–204.

Hart, B., Sainsbury, P. and Short, S. (1998). Whose dying? A sociological critique of a "good death". *Mortality*, 3(1), 65–77.

Hockings, J. (1988). *Walking the Tightrope, Living Positively With AIDS, ARC and HIV*. Loughton, Gale Centre Publications.

Hope, J. (1990). Can there really be life after death? *The Daily Mail*, 5 October 1990.

Ivan, L. and Melrose, M. (1986). *The Way We Die*. Chichester, Angel Press.

Kastenbaum, R. (1998). *Death, Society and Human Experience*, 6th edn. Boston, Allyn and Bacon.

Kirmayer, L.J. (1992). The body's insistence on meaning, metaphor as presentation and representation in illness experience. *Medical Anthropology Quarterly* 6(4), 323–46.

Laine, C. & Davidoff. F. (1996). Patient-centred medicine: a professional evolution. *Journal of the Americnl Medical Association*, 275,152–56.

Marsh, I. and Keating, M. (2006). *Sociology: Making Sense of Society*, 3rd edn. Harlow, Prentice Hall.

Neuberger, J. and White, J.A. (1991). *A Necessary End: Attitudes to Death*. London, Macmillan.

Office of National Statistics (2007). *Death registrations in 2005*. Available at: http://www.statistics.gov.uk/CCI/nugget.asp?ID = 952&Pos = &ColRank = 1&Rank = 374 (last accessed February 2009).

Parsons, T. (1951). *The Social System*. New York, Free Press.

Sabom, M. (1982). *Recollections of Death: A Medical Investigation*. New York, Harper and Row.

Scott, T. (1990). Just a few months. In: H. Alexander (ed.). *Living with Dying*. London, BBC Publications.

Seymour, J. and Clark, D. (1998). Phenomenological approaches to palliative care research. *Palliative Medicine*, 12, 127–31.

Stone, A. (1977). *The Owl and the Nightingale*. Harmondsworth, Penguin.

Thomas, D. (1963). *Miscellany One*. Letchworth, Hants, Aldine Press.

Toates, F. (1999). Human consciousness and the near-death experience. *SK220 Human Biology and Health* (Offprint III). Milton Keynes, The Open University.

Wanless, D. (2004). *Securing Good Health for the Whole Population: Final Report* Norwich, HMSO.

Weisman, A. (1972). *On Dying and Denying*. New York, Behavioural Publications.

Widgery, D. (1993). Not going gently. In: D. Dickinson and M. Johnson (eds). *Death, Dying and Bereavement*, 1st edn. London, Sage, pp. 16–20.

World Health Organization (1977). *Conquering Suffering, Enriching Humanity*. Geneva, WHO.

Chapter 6
Developments in end-of-life care

June L. Leishman

Past all your knowing
I shall be going
To far-away kingdoms
Soon, Soon …

From *Song* by W.H. Auden (1907–1973)

Introduction

The concept of a good death is the central focus of both hospice and palliative care, to ensure that people who are terminally ill progress through their illness trajectory with as little discomfort and as much dignity as possible. The opportunity to die with dignity is recognised by health professionals the world over as one of the most fundamental of all human rights. However, Walter (2003) reminds us that the concept of the good death has changed in different cultures and societies throughout history and in particular in Western societies, dominated by religion in the past, and medicine in the present. Notions of a good death vary considerably between cultures as well as between individuals within a culture, raising the risk of misunderstanding and cultural insensitivity when caring for people at the end of their lives. Not only has the UK become a much older society, in terms of its age distribution, but also a more multicultural society, as reflected in the diversity of beliefs and value systems that derive from the traditions of all the cultural groupings it encompasses. Thus, issues of ageing, illness, religion, tradition, kinship, ethnicity, science, medical care and morality become germane in our conceptions, experiences and depictions of death and dying, at both a societal and an individual level. Dominant religious beliefs in any society or ethnic or religious community have a deep effect on attitudes to death and dying, and we can see a continuance of traditional customs and practices in immigrant and migrant communities in the UK that hark back to their past in their home countries before the diasporas. Firth's (1993) study of Hindu and Sikh approaches to death in Asian communities in the United Kingdom emphasises the importance of culturally sensitive end-of-life care.

In the UK, the welfare state has sought to provide care from cradle to grave. Yet according to Clark (1999) in the first two decades of the National Health Service there was little evidence of strategies or operational guidance for the care of the dying. He further notes that, paradoxically, the independent modern hospice movement arose beneath the shadow of this new and inclusive system of health care (although it should be noted that hospices did exist before this point). Palliative care has had a similar journey to the hospice movement in relation to its long history and transition since the establishment of the NHS.

Places where people die are as diverse as dying itself. People die in their own homes or in communities. Dying can be short, either following an emergency health situation such as stroke or heart failure, or as a result of accident or other trauma. Or it can be long and lingering, as experienced by those with terminal illnesses. For some, their end of life may take place en route to hospital, for others it may be in prisons, hostels or other centres of detention. It is not uncommon for an individual to have no choice in where they die and to have no say in how they are cared for during the dying process and at the end of their lives. For many people who are ill in modern Western society, hospitals or nursing homes are the most common dying places, and will likely continue to be in the future. However, it is in hospices and in the provision of palliative care that beacons of excellence in end-of-life care have developed through time. They have been the flagships of caring for dying people and supporting their relatives for many years. It is within these two areas of Westernised health care that education and training in end-of-life care and the origins of death education for health-care professionals has its roots.

The need for health services to respond to ethnic and cultural diversity in the UK has emerged as a significant issue in both policy and service development (Adunsky *et al.,* 1999). However, in a study of a London hospice Guneratnam (1993) noted that it was founded by a group of white Christian professionals. At the time of her study, although the hospice served a diverse mix of ethnic minorities, and despite there being no ethnic minority staff, no groups were discriminated against on the grounds of their ethnicity by the doctors, senior nurses or senior managers of the hospice. Hospices have Christian roots and largely female spiritually oriented leaders and some cultural groups do not view them as the most appropriate places to care for dying people. This accounts for the limited uptake of services in this area of care provision for minority ethnic groups (O'Neill, 1994; Neuberger, 1994; Hill and Penso, 1995; Henley and Schott, 1999; Gatrad *et al.*, 2003). Indeed, Clark (1993; p. 14) goes so far as to say:

> "There are general questions about the extent to which the hospice model is taking account of a range of social differences relating to gender, age, sexuality, family circumstances, religion and ethnicity … Too often hospices appear as white, middle-class Christian institutions serving a carefully selected group of patients, which the odour of goodness (Smith, 1984) surrounding them cannot fail to disguise."

While it is fair to say that service provision has moved on since the publication of Clark's work, the discussions that follow echo concerns that the historical philosophical premise on which both hospices and palliative care were founded remain constant, and within that constancy the needs of all cultural groups may not be met. Powell *et al.* (2003, p. 23) note that if hospices are too focused on originality, autonomy and control … dying with dignity might be about being fragile and dependent upon others. This is not a concept that is subscribed in all cultures.

Perspectives on death and dying

The hospice movement

The hospice movement

According to the *Oxford English Dictionary*, a hospice is "a home for people who are ill (esp. terminally) or destitute; a lodging for travellers (esp. one kept by a religious order)". Modern hospices are rooted in deep and ancient traditions of compassionate care going back to the earliest civilisations. Ancient hospices contained a broad spread of the diseased, poor and down-trodden, and cared for them over a long period of time. The ancient history of hospice care can be traced back to St Fabiola in the 4th century, who cared for and nursed the sick and dying. Fabiola was a member of a wealthy Roman partisan family. Following the death of her second consort, she made the decision to enter into a life of caring for others. She became a Christian ascetic, a person who practises severe self-discipline and abstains from any form of pleasure, for religious or spiritual reasons. She sold all her belongings and used her wealth to found the first hospital in the Western world, in Rome. Despite her aristocratic heritage, she was known for treating patients herself, even those whose wounds and injuries were so repulsive that they would have been rejected by others. However, we should be cautious about seeing her as someone who prefigured the charismatic leaders of the modern hospice approach developed in the second half of the 20th century; her journey into this new life of care and the sisterhood began as a penance following a rather colourful beginning. Fabiola continued living this way until her death and was awarded a sainthood by the Pope in recognition of her dedication to caring for the sick and dying.

More recent history reveals the first concentrated efforts to give institutional care to dying people. The 19th century saw the building of large numbers of hospitals. This led to a lessening of concern for people at the end of their lives with conditions that were beyond cure. At this point in time, both the bereaved and the medical establishment considered the first signs of death to be a medical failure. By the 1950s, social trends were changing and most Western-oriented people were dying in hospitals rather than their own homes. This change reflected the growing number of treatments available in hospitals. The medical profession increasingly saw death as failure, and cancer was the most feared diagnosis. Physical pain afflicted at least three-quarters of cancer sufferers and appropriate painkillers were rarely used. Morphine was considered addictive and too dangerous to use in large doses, so prescription for pain relief was less than satisfactory.

The three primary patient concerns that hospice care directly addresses are the difficulties associated with pain management, the fear of having other people controlling one's life, and the loneliness and fear of death (Mango, 1990). Kubler-Ross (1969) reminds us that for many people, death is a fearful, frightening prospect that can cause distressing experiences for the patient and his or her family; *fearful* because it brings one face to face with mortality and permanent separation from one's loved ones. Central to the goals of hospice care is the promotion of autonomy for both patient and family and ensuring that the quality of life provided before death is as good as it can be, with support given to the patient and family throughout the dying process. It is also evident that care by these early pioneers of end-of-life care is based on a mainly Western Christian script.

In the UK and Ireland in the 1960s there were a few long-established Catholic hospices, ten Marie Curie homes and nineteen beds allocated for the terminal care of cancer patients (James and Field, 1992). Dame Cicely Saunders founded St Christopher's hospice in England in 1967. It was not the first hospice in Britain, but it made an extraordinary contribution to alleviating human suffering. St Christopher's is regarded symbolically as the beginning of the modern hospice movement. Cicely Saunders, with degrees in nursing, social work and medicine, and a confirmed Christian, was well qualified for her work. Hospices have been centres of innovation and insight since they were first established. Under the leadership of Cicely Saunders, St Christopher's set out to find practical solutions in the care of the dying and disseminated these widely. The term hospice was specifically chosen by institutions caring for the terminally ill to evoke both the medieval way-station for spiritual travellers and to differentiate them from ordinary hospitals (Schneidman, 1984). The Christian underpinning of the movement was reflected by the use of Saints' names. Much is documented about Cicely Saunders, in her own notes and in interviews with others, and she continues to sit alongside other champions of the hospice movement (Du Boulay, 1884; Cassidy, 1988; Saunders, 1988).

Perspectives on death and dying

A major aspect of what makes us human is our need to make sense of life, by plotting our mark on our cultural map, of which ethnicity is a key feature. Hospice philosophy is rooted in accepting death as a stage in life, in contrast to modern medicine whose efforts, as one might expect, are based on models of care and interventions that seek to cure or prevent death (Kellehear, 2005). No tradition should be reduced to a few sentences. Death arouses great curiosity. Questions about the meaning and the purpose of life are coupled with questions about what comes next. When carers know little about other people's sensitivities and values, the quality of experience they offer may be impoverished and lead to people in their care feeling marginalised and insignificant.

The philosophy of hospice care is general and holistic. For some people, hospice care has become synonymous with care of people with terminal cancer. It has allowed the development of a model of care that is highly specialised and this has been the strength in the sustainability of hospices over time. The hospice movement has now become part of mainstream health care and an influential player in health-care policy and politics in many parts of the world. In particular, hospices have shown that cancer symptoms, especially pain, can be controlled without negative side effects. This has been achieved in part by single-minded determination to provide pain-free, holistic, client-centred care.

Howarth (2007) proposes that hospice care neither hastens nor postpones death. Rather it affirms life and regards dying as normal (which is central to many cultural beliefs). By accepting death as normal, hospice care seeks to give dying patients and their families dignity, by supporting them as they come to terms with difficult concepts in what can be very complicated circumstances. They also create a relaxed and comfortable environment for the dying person, which allows family and friends to be close and helps them provide emotional support as a means of meeting the dying person's social and emotional needs. In so doing, the quality of life through the dying process for the dying person is enhanced.

However, hospice care varies with cultural diversity in some ways. In studying Japanese cancer care, Hirai *et al.* (2003) citeseventeen components of what constitutes a good death in Japan.

Developments in end-of-life care

These are shared with common components of a good death in Western countries, and include factors such as family support, dignity, preparation for death and pain management. However, they also identify the Japanese model of *omakase* (trusting) as being unique to that culture, whereby patients place total trust in professional decision making; it is normal for Japanese people to participate fully in their treatment because they feel the doctor knows best. The Buddhist philosophy of compassion, wisdom, doing no harm, willingness to serve and the significance of death also appears to sit comfortably with hospice discourse (McGrath, 1998). However, religious and spiritual discourses on dying – such as those in Buddhism, Confuscianism and Shinto – take a different form from the Christian assumptions that frame these discussions in the West, and they challenge Western notions of medicalisation and sequestration of the dying that are embedded within hospice care (Long, 1999; Harvey, 2000).

Dame Saunders' philosophy was that hospice patients should live until they die. By that she meant that they should be encouraged to enjoy hobbies and other meaningful activities and that the hospice team should make necessary accommodations for them to do so. Thus it also implies that the roles of the members of the multidisciplinary team need to be flexible, innovative and accommodating of individual patient choice, as a means of ensuring that their time until death is as fulfilling as possible. Greene (1984) identifies the role of the nurse in this situation as someone who helps the hospice patient to live each day as fully and autonomously as possible. Greene (1984) further notes that nurses must make daily assessments of what the patient is capable of doing and work with the patient to decide what support is needed. The rationale is that each day might be different for each patient because the disease progression varies from person to person; therefore daily assessment and patient involvement contribute to the provision of high-quality care, which is at the very heart of hospice care. Traditionally, hospice funding reflects its philanthropic history in that many hospices remain charitable organisations. However, across the sector within the UK funding varies from 100 per cent funding by the NHS to almost 100 per cent funding by charitable trusts, although the service is always free to patients.

Perspectives on death and dying

The first hospices in Ireland and Scotland

Hospices in Ireland and Scotland

The origins of both Ireland and Scotland's first hospices can be traced back to a woman called Mary Aitkenhead, from Cork, who was both a feminist and a pioneer. She was a member of the Anglican Communion until the age of fifteen when she converted to Roman Catholicism.

Our Lady's Hospice in Dublin and St Margaret's Hospice in Scotland were established by the Congregation of the Religious of Charity founded by Mary Aitkenhead in 1815. At that time the incidence of tuberculosis in Dublin was twice that of London and Glasgow; the incidence of typhoid and measles was three times greater than in London; and Dublin had the highest death rate of any continent or North American City, topped only by Calcutta in 1989.

Our Lady's hospice in Dublin was open to all religions and classes and its admissions were for disease, poverty, starvation and helplessness. The first medical doctor to work in the hospice was Dr Dudley White who was appointed there in 1879. He was followed by a distinguished body of physicians and visiting physicians. From the beginning there was a drive to be at the forefront of care. In 1961, the country's first geriatrician, Dr John Fleetwood, was appointed to the hospice. As the 1950s ended there was a change in the conditions from which patients suffered. The scourge of tuberculosis, from which many hospice patients suffered, was being overcome and there was an increase in the number of patients with cancer. Today, Our Lady's hospice cares for over 1,500 patients and, in conjunction with the University of Dublin, offers teaching and practical experience for doctors, nurses and other professions allied to medicine.

In Scotland, St Margaret's Hospice (as it was known since 1950) has changed its name to St Margaret of Scotland Hospice. Queen Margaret of Scotland was born in southern Hungary, in the village of Mecseknadas, probably in Castle Reka. She was the grand-daughter of the English king, Edmund Ironside. Margaret enjoyed her privileged position and great wealth, but regarded herself merely as the steward of riches. She lived in a spirit of inward poverty, looking on nothing as her own; everything she possessed was to be used for the purposes of God. Margaret's great influence was in the care of the poor and in charity. She founded several churches including the Abbey of Dunfermline. She was a great philanthropist who was raised to saintly status because of her charitable work. Fifty years ago a Sister of Charity, newly arrived in Clydebank to help with the work of the parish and school, was approached by a gentleman with advanced throat cancer. He told her that he had nowhere to go and did not know what to do as his condition was worsening and he had no-one to care for him. As a result, the Sister contacted Dublin and asked if it might be possible for them to send over a Sister who was trained in nursing to look after this man and others like him. All the houses in the congregation tried to raise money to send a Sister to Clydebank. With the help of the local churches and community, sufficient money was found to buy a house and establish a small hospice. Thus it began, and grew steadily as demand arose.

Evidence of the strong Catholic history of hospice care is seen in the expansion of hospice developments across the world. St Joseph's Hospice Association in Liverpool supports hospices in Guatemala, Honduras, Ecuador and Peru, as well as having links with hospices in Pakistan, India and Mexico that bear the same name. Other faiths have recognised the need for high-quality specialised end-of-life care for people with terminal illness, leading to global developments in this area (Clark *et al.*, 2007).

Throughout the history of the hospice movement, end-of-life care has focused on the adult population, with little care available for children or young adults. Only in the 1980s were developments seen in this area in the UK. The following examples highlight the need for high-quality care for young people, as they and their families struggle with terminal illness.

Hospices for children

Hospices for children

Helen House was the world's first children's hospice. It opened in England in November 1982, as a result of a friendship between Sister Frances Dominica and the parents of a seriously ill child called Helen. Helen lived at home with her family but required round-the-clock care and the experiences of her family highlighted the need for respite care and support for children with life-shortening conditions. Thus Helen House was set up to help families cope by providing occasional respite care modelled on that provided in the family home and tailored to the child's individual needs. Helen House continues to provide respite and end-of-life care in a supportive and positive environment, and is staffed by a multiskilled team of professionals.

Rachel House was Scotland's first children's hospice. It opened in 1996 in Kinross, Fife. It is purpose built and provides ongoing support for up to 200 families from across Scotland each year. At any one time, it can accommodate eight children and their families. Around 1,200 families in Scotland have a child or children who suffer from a progressive, life-limiting condition. Most are unlikely to live to adulthood.

Interdisciplinarity is the cornerstone of effective hospice care. Members of the hospice multidisciplinary team include doctors, nurses, chaplains, social workers, physiotherapists and occupational therapists (Buckingham, 1996; Lawton, 2000). Rhodes *et al.* (2008) studied factors that influence overall satisfaction with care. They found that bereaved family members were almost four times more likely to rate their satisfaction with services as excellent if they were kept informed about their loved one's condition than if they were not informed. Seale (1998) supports a client-centred approach to hospice care, with particular emphasis on participation of families as well as care tailored to the specific needs of each patient. He stresses that involvement of both patients and family members in decision-making contributes to overall satisfaction with hospice service provision, and in turn contributes to patient well-being.

Hospice care and palliative care have a shared history. The evolution of one into the other has occurred over time, developing a model of care that has benefited many people at the end of their lives.

Palliative care: a journey through time

Palliative care

The first reference to palliative care dates back to Hippocrates around 460 BC. Modern historical pioneers of early palliative care are Jeanne Garnier of France and Mary Aitkenhead of Ireland (David, 2000). Although these two women never met, they shared a common goal in their concern for the care of the dying and the poor. Previously we acknowledged Mary Aitkenhead's influence on the introduction of hospice care in the UK and Ireland. Similarly, Jeanne Garnier was born in Lyon in 1811. Her influence led to the founding of six establishments for care of the dying between 1853 and her death in Paris in 1874. Within three years of marriage, she suffered the death of two children and her husband. Together with some other widows she founded L'Association des Dames du Cavaire in 1842. A home for the dying opened the following year. The philosophy of care in the homes established under her influence was one of Christian prayer and calm in the face of death in addition to respectfulness. Like many institutions in these times, medical and nursing care were very unsophisticated, so they were simply committed to providing spiritual, moral and humanely supportive care, with a deeply religious base.

As the Western world encountered the two world wars, the social structure of society shifted. Some important developments in medicine and health care were also emerging – a greater emphasis on cure and rehabilitation, medical specialisations, more deaths taking place in hospitals rather than in homes, and a change in attitudes to death and dying. At this time, Cicely Saunders was publishing her first paper on care of the dying, and the writings of Kubler-Ross revived optimism about what could be achieved in caring for dying patients (Kubler-Ross, 1969). This was a time of innovation in end-of-life care, and a time to rethink and reorganise and deliver end-of-life care (Hockey, 1997; Saunders and Kastenbaum, 1997). In 1990 the World Health Organization (WHO) defined palliative care as the active total care of patients for a disease that is not responsive to curative treatment including control of pain, other symptoms, and psychological, social and spiritual problems.

It espouses an approach that improves the quality of life of patients and their families through the process of dying, and at death itself. Palliative care neither aims to hasten nor postpone dying. It is concerned primarily with symptom relief and an approach to care that embraces the holistic concept of spiritual, psychological and social comfort. The UK Government's white paper *Our Health, Our Care, Our Say* highlights the importance of ensuring that all health professionals who work with people who are dying are properly trained to look after dying patients and their families. It also promises to roll out frameworks such as the Liverpool Care Pathway (LCP) across the country as a means of facilitating this. The Specialist Palliative Care team at the Royal Liverpool and Broadgreen University Hospitals NHS Trust and the Marie Curie Hospice in Liverpool developed the LCP. It has been recognised as a model of best practice and was recommended in the National Institute for Clinical Excellence (NICE) guidance on supportive and palliative care for patients with cancer (NICE, 2004). The aims of the LCP are to improve care of the dying in the last hours or days of life; it is designed to improve knowledge about the process of dying and provide high-quality end-of-life care. Although initially intended for use with cancer patients, the LCP has been adapted and disseminated across a range of care settings and has been used in many other terminal conditions. It provides guidance on key aspects of care such as:

- symptom control
- comfort measures
- anticipatory prescribing of medication
- discontinuation of inappropriate interventions
- psychological and spiritual care
- care of the family before and after the death of the patient.

The LCP has been adapted to illnesses other than cancer, including heart failure and renal failure, and for use in intensive care units and for children (Liverpool Care Pathway, 2007). In part, this serves the needs of people with other terminal illnesses, including migrant communities, who have proportionately higher death rates from diseases other than cancer.

Faull *et al.* (2005; p. 74) estimate that 56 million people across the world die each year, with 80 per cent of these in developing countries. It is in these countries that a multiplicity of challenges such as poverty, ageing, cancer and HIV/AIDS challenge palliative care. There seems to be little training of health-care professionals in transcultural medicine and therefore no opportunity to learn the death rites of different cultures. In a preliminary review of qualitative literature in Britain on a diversities approach to end-of-life care, Jones (2005) warns against a 'cookbook' approach to diversity; it is claimed that this creates new myths and/or stereotypes, compounded by inaccuracies or misunderstandings. Jones further suggests that the time has arrived when parochial views, practices and concepts in end-of-life care will no longer suffice in a multi-cultural/racial/ethnic global society. If for no other reason, the swift exchange of information and practice now possible on a global scale makes narrow and regional/local methodologies obsolete.

New developments in the UK

New developments

In July 2008, the UK Government published its End-of-Life Care Strategy promoting high-quality end-of-life care for all adults. This is the first strategy of its kind in the UK and at present it covers adults in England. Its aim is to provide people approaching the end of life with more choice about where they would like to live and die in the time leading to their death. It encompasses all adults with advanced, progressive illness and applies to all care settings. The strategy has been developed by an expert advisory board chaired by Professor Mike Richards, the National Cancer Director, and including key stakeholders from statutory health, social care and third-sector organisations, professionals and academic organisers. The strategy has been informed and shaped by the work on end-of-life care undertaken by strategic health authorities for the NHS Next Stage Review, which acknowledged that people who are nearing the end of their lives need care for 24 hours per day and that even where services are available, they do not always meet the individual needs of the dying person and their family. It also acknowledges that at times there are difficulties providing appropriate care for people with complex physical problems, mental health problems and learning disabilities. It looks at care pathways, adopting the death trajectories model, and the strategy takes a six-step approach to end-of-life care that includes:

(1) discussions as the end of life approaches

(2) assessment, care planning and review

(3) coordination of care for the individual patient

(4) delivery of high-quality care in different settings

(5) care in the last days of life, and

(6) care after death.

Alongside this care plan for patients, the Government proposes care and support for families by providing them with information, and spiritual support. The proposed care pathway is illustrated below.

Table 6.1 **The end-of-life care plan for supporting carers and families throughou,t before, during and after the death of their loved one (adapted from Department of Health, 2008)**

Step 1	Discussion as end of life approaches	Open and honest communication
		Identify triggers for discussion
Step 2	Assessment, care planning, review	Agree care plan and regularly review needs and preferences
		Assess needs of carers
Step 3	Coordination of care	Strategic coordination
		Coordinate individual patient care
		Rapid response services
Step 4	Delivery of high-quality services	High-quality care provision in all settings (hospitals, community, care homes, hospices, prisons, secure hospitals, hostels, ambulance services)
Step 5	Care in last days of life	Identify the dying phase
		Review needs and preferences for place of death
		Support patients and carers
		Recognise wishes about resuscitation and organ/tissue donation
Step 6	Care after death	Recognise that end-of-life care does not stop at point of death
		Verify and certify the death timely[?] or refer to coroner
		Provide care and practical and emotional support for carers and family

Consideration is also given to different types of death. It suggests that for deaths that are short and acute, steps (5) and (6) would be appropriate; for sudden deaths step (6) would be the most appropriate. A strategic coordinated approach to implementing the plan is proposed, which will bring together all services from the NHS, local authorities and voluntary, independent sector to work in partnership with each other, with the LCP proposed as the recommended guidance for end-of-life care and for care after death for bereaved families.

Recognition is given to the fact that the specialist palliative-care workforce is relatively small and that the total number of health- and social-care professionals who deliver end-of-life care is huge, if all staff working in those areas covered at the outset of this discussion are included. It is clear from the literature that many staff at all levels receive little or no training or continuing professional development in end-of-life care. It is also clear that there is a need for health-care professionals to have culturally sensitive health-care education. This new strategy is welcome, but following publication there will also need to be consideration of the provision of high-quality end-of-life care across all settings and by all professionals associated with dying patients, and their families, across the other nations of the UK. Supporting data is available on places of death and causes of death, but little is available on individual choice about where to die or care provision. The new strategy therefore proposes that better use is made of existing data sources and, more innovatively, supports the establishment of a national end-of-life care intelligence network, designed to bring together owners of data and people with interest and expertise in this area.

Conclusions

A diagnosis of cancer, heart disease, or even AIDS, does not necessarily mean that a person will die. Medical advances in recent years have created a population of people diagnosed with serious illness who are living with dying. They may live for many years with their condition before dying and hospices are adapting to this changing environment. Howarth and Leamen (2001) argued that the challenge for hospices is to provide care for patients suffering from other disease conditions such as dementia, chronic obstructive pulmonary disease, and AIDS. They further argue that another challenge is to reach out to other parts of the world that have a greater need for symptom control and end-of-life care. This view is supported by Clark *et al.* (2007); fuller evidence concerning palliative care provision is needed than presently exists in the countries of Africa. The results of their study show that 21 out of 47 countries have no palliative or hospice activity in place. There is also a low level of opioid use for the management of pain in the countries that do have hospices.

The UK Government's End-of-Life Care Strategy looks positively to the future within the UK, although it makes several key suggestions for improvement in taking this initiative forward. The strategic plan reminds us that the UK makes a considerable contribution to worldwide research on end-of-life care – but it could do better. It also highlights the importance of education and training for health-care professionals as being key to the delivery of high-quality end-of-life care. We will all be affected in some way by death, regardless of our culture, religion, or other differentiating factors. It is thereforehoped that the discussions, debates and dilemmas mentioned in this paper will stimulate thinking about death, dying and end-of-life care from a multicultural standpoint.

Reflective questions

1. How would you differentiate between hospice care and palliative care?

2. What would be your priorities in providing support to bereaved families after the death of their loved one?

3. Identify four challenges that hospices may be faced with in today's society.

4. What are your views on the UK Government's proposed new end-of-life strategy?

References and further reading

Ahrens, J. (2005). The positive impact of hospice care on the surviving spouse. *Home Health Nurse*, 23(1), 53–55.

Adunsky, A., Hall, R., Girsh, F. and Enck, R.E. (1999). Letter to the editor.

American Journal of Hospice and Palliative Care, 16, 442–44.

Buckingham, R. (1996). *The Handbook of Hospice Care*. New York, Prometheus Books.

Cassidy, S. (1988). Emotional distress in terminal cancer: discussion paper. *Journal of the Royal Society of Medicine*, **79**(12), 717–20.

Charlton, R. (2002). *Primary Palliative Care: Dying, Death and Bereavement in the Community*. Oxon, Radcliffe Medical Press.

Christakis, N. and Iwashna, T. (2003). The health impact of health care on families: a matched cohort study of hospice use by descendants and mortality outcomes in surviving widowed spouses. *Social Science and Medicine*, **57**(3), 465–75.

Clark, D. (1993). Originating a movement: Cicely Saunders and the development of St. Christopher's Hospice. *Mortality*, **3**(1), 43–63.

Clark, D. (1999). Terminal care in the United Kingdom 1948–1967 *Mortality*, **4** (3) pp. 225–247.

Clark, D. and Wright, M. (2007). The International Observatory on End-of-Life Care: A global view of palliative care development. *Journal of Pain and Symptom Management*, **33**(5), 542–46.

Clark, D., Wright, M., Hunt, J. and Lynch, T. (2007). Hospice and palliative care development in Africa: a multi-method review of services and experiences. *Journal of Pain and Symptom Management*, **33**(6), 698–710.

Connor, S., Pyenson, B., Fitch, K., Spence, C. and Iwasaki, K. (2007). Comparing hospice and non-hospice patient survival among patients who die within a three-year window. *Journal of Pain and Symptom Management*, **33**(3), 238–46.

Corr, C., Nabe, C. and Corr, D. (2003). *Death and Dying. Life and Living*. London, Thomson Warworth.

Department of Health (2008). *End-of-Life Care Strategy*. London, Department of Health.

Du Boulay, S., (1984). *Cicely Saunders: Founder of the Modern Hospice Movement*. London, Hodder and Stoughton.

Faull, C., Carter, Y. and Daniels, L. (2005). *Handbook of Palliative Care*. Edinburgh, Blackwell.

Fine, P. and Davis, M. (2006). Hospice: comprehensive care at the end of life. *Anaesthesiology Clinics of North America*, **24**(1), 181–204.

Firth, S. (1993). Approaches to death in Hindu and Sikh communities in Britain. In: D. Dickenson and M. Johnson (eds). *Death, Dying and Bereavement*. Milton Keynes, The Open University.

Foggo, B. (2006). The hospice: A place to die or just passing on? *Progress in Palliative Care*, **14**(3), 109–111.

Gatrad, A.R., Brown, E., Notta, H. and Sheikh, A. (2003). Palliative care needs for minorities. *British Medical Journal*, **327**, 176–79.

Graham, F. and Clarke, D. (2008). The changing model of palliative care. *Medicine* **36**(2), 64–66.

Greene, P. (1984). The pivotal role of a nurse in hospice care. *A Cancer Journal for Clinicians*, **34**, 204–05.

Guneratnam, Y. (1993). Breaking the silence: Asian carers in Britain. In: J. Bornat *et al.* (eds). *Community Care: A Reader*. London, Macmillan.

Harai, K., Miyashita, M., Morita, T., Sanjo, M. and Uchitomi, Y. (2003). Good death in Japanese cancer care: A qualitative study. *Journal of Pain and Symptom Management*, 31(2), 140–47.

Harvey, P. (2000). *An Introduction to Buddhist Ethics: Foundations, Values and Issues*. Cambridge, Cambridge University Press.

Henley, A. and Schott, J. (1999). *Culture, Religion and Patient Care in a Multi-Ethnic Society*. London, Age Concern England.

Hill, D. and Penso, D. (1995). Opening doors: improving access to hospice and palliative care services by members of the black and ethnic communities. *British Medical Journal*, 301, 277–81.

Hirai,K., Moita, T. and Kashiwagi, T. (2003). Professionally perceived effectiveness of psychosocial interventions for existential suffering of terminally ill cancer patients. *Palliative Medicine*, 17(8), 688–94.

Hockey, N. (1997). Palliative care ethics: a good companion. *Journal of Medical Ethics*, 23, 259.

Howarth, G. (2007). *Death and Dying: A Sociological Introduction*. Cambridge, Polity.

Howarth, G. and Leamen, O. (2001). *Encyclopaedia of Death and Dying*. London, Routledge.

James, V. and Field, D. (1992). The routinization of hospice: charisma and bureaucratization. *Social Science and Medicine*, 34(12), 1363–75.

Jones, K. (2005). Diversities in approach to end-of-life: A view from Britain of the qualitative literature. *Journal of Research in Nursing*, 10(4), 431–45.

Kastenbaum, R. (2001). *Death, Society and Human Experience*. London, Allyn and Bacon.

Kellehear (2005). *Compassionate Cities: Public Health and End-of-Life Care*, New York, Routledge.

Kubler-Ross, E. (1969). *On Death and Dying*. New York, Macmillan.

Lawton, J. (2000). *The Dying Process: Patients' Experiences of Palliative Care*. Florence, Routledge.

Liverpool Care Pathway (2007). *Non-Cancer Briefing Paper*. Liverpool, LCP Central Team.

Long, S.O. (1999) (ed.). *Lives in Motion: Composing Circles of a Self and Community in Japan*. Ithaca, Cornell East Asia Series.

Long, S.O. (2004). Cultural scripts for a good death in Japan and the United States: Similarities and differences. *Journal of Social Sciences and Medicine*, 56(5), 913–28.

Mango, J. (1990). The hospice concept of care: facing the 1990s. *Death Studies*, 4(2), 109–19.

McGrath, P. (1998). Buddhist spirituality – a compassionate perspective on hospice care. *Mortality*, 3(3), 251–64.

National Institute for Clinical Excellence (2004). 2004/015 New guidance will improve supportive and palliative care services for adults with cancer.

Available at: http://www.nice.org.uk/newsevents/pressreleases/pressre-leasearchive/pressreleases2004/2004_015_new_guidance_will_improve_support ive_and_palliative_care_services_for_adults_with_cancer.jsp (last accessed February 2009).

Neuberger, J. (1994). *Caring for Dying People of Different Faiths*. London, Mosby.

O'Brien, T.A. (2007). Overseas nurses in the National Health Service: A process of deskilling. *Journal of Clinical Nursing*, 16(12), 2229–36.

O'Neill, J. (1994). Ethnic minorities – neglected by palliative care providers? *Journal of Cancer Care*, 3, 215–20.

Poor, B. and Polirne, G. (2001). *End of Life Nursing Care*. London, Jones Bartlett.

Powell, L.H., Shahabi, L. and Thorensen, C.E. (2003). Religion and spirituality: linkages to physical health. *American Psychologist*, 58, 36–52.

Praill, D. (2000). Who are we here for? *Palliative Medicine*, 14, 91–92.

Quill, T. (2001). *Caring for Patients at the End of Life Facing an Uncertain Future*. Oxford, Oxford University Press.

Rhodes, R., Mitchell, S., Miller, S., Connor, S. and Teno, J. (2008). Bereaved family members' evaluation of hospice care: What factors influence overall satisfaction with services? *Journal of Pain and Symptom Management*, 35(4), 1–7.

Saunders, C. (1988). Spiritual pain. *Journal of Palliative Care*, 4(3), 29–32.

Saunders, C. and Kastenbaum, R. (1997). *Hospice Care on the International Scene*. New York: Springer.

Scottish Executive (2003). *National care standards: Hospice care*. Available at: http://www.scotland.gov.uk/Resource/Doc/46737/0013960.pdf (last accessed February 2009).

Seale, C. (1998). *Constructing Death: The Sociology of Dying and Bereavement*. Cambridge, Cambridge University Press.

Smith, M.D, McSweeney, M. and Katz, B.M. (1980). Characteristics of death education curricula in American medical schools. *Journal of Medical Education*, 55(10), 844–50.

UN AIDS (2005). *AIDS in Africa: Three scenarios to 2025*. Available at: http://data.unaids.org/publications/IRC-pub07/jc1058-aidsinafrica_en.pdf (last accessed 20 February 2009).

Walter, C.A. (2003). *Loss of a Life Partner: Narratives of the Bereaved*. New York, Columbia University Press.

Websites of interest

St Joseph's Hospital Association, Liverpool

http://www.jospice.org.uk/oseas.htm

St Margaret of Scotland Hospice

http://www.smh.org.uk

Chapter 7
Death and the challenge of ageing
June L. Leishman

I warm'd both hands before the fire of Life:
It sinks; and I am ready to depart.

From *The Dying Speech of an Old Philosopher* by Walter Savage Landor
(1775–1864)

Introduction

Death is one certainty we all face in our lives. Although the timing and nature of death is uncertain, it becomes more imminent as we grow older. We have already discussed how death engenders complex feelings and responses that contribute to the challenges faced when caring for those at the end of their lives. Different people have different views of the transition from life to death, and the way in which that transition is accepted, managed and experienced is also different for every person. This influences the priorities that older people have about dying, their dying process and the places they wish to die in. In the Western world, we live in a society where longevity has increased. According to the World Health Organization, the number of people in the world aged over 60 is expected to double by the year 2050; 10 to 20 per cent of these will be from "rich" countries and 18 to 35 per cent from "poor" countries. By 2020 the chief causes of death among the population are expected to be chronic illnesses such as heart disease, cerebrovascular disease, chronic respiratory infections and lung cancer. Ageing is a privilege and a societal achievement. It is also a challenge, and it will impact on all aspects of 21st-century society. In the developed world, the very old (80 years or more) is the fastest-growing population group. Women outlive men in virtually all societies; consequently in very old age the ratio of women to men is two to one.

Many among our ageing population have experienced two world wars and a myriad of social changes. Although the UK population grew by 8 per cent in 35 years (from 55.9 million in 1971 to 60.6 million in 2006), this change did not occur evenly across all age groups (see Fig. 7.1). The population aged over 65 grew by 31 per cent (from 7.4 to 9.7 million) while the population aged under 16 declined by 19 per cent (from 14.2 to 11.5 million). The largest percentage growth in population in the year to mid-2006 was seen at ages 85 and over (5.9 per cent). The number of people aged 85 and over grew by 69,000 in the year to mid-2006, reaching a record 1.2 million. This large increase reflects improved survival and the post-World War I baby-boomers.

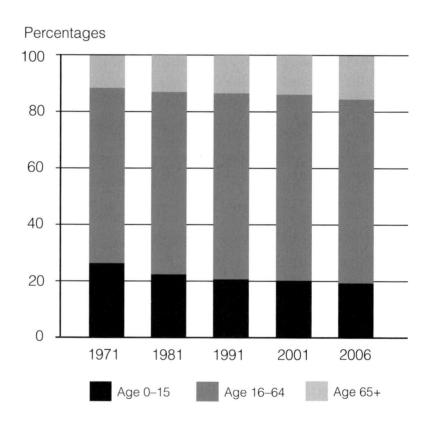

Fig. 7.1 **The changing age structure of the UK population, 1971–2006**

Death and the challenge of ageing

While many of these old people live active and healthy lives, there is no doubt that at some time they will die. Poor health in the elderly is often the result of an accumulation of a lifetime of risk factors such as high blood pressure, smoking, alcohol consumption and poor diet. Other issues, such as reduced mobility, eyesight problems and mental health problems, actively contribute to their vulnerability (WHO, 2004). As there is a significantly large ageing population today, it seems relevant to look at the ways in which older people in contemporary society make sense of death, both their own and that of others. Although the majority of deaths occur in later life, there has been little research into their needs at the end of their lives. The World Health Organization (WHO, 2004) identify that older people may have different and more complex needs because:

- They are most commonly affected by multiple medical problems.
- The cumulative effect of these may be greater than any individual disease.
- They are at a greater risk of adverse drug reactions and of iatrogenic illness.
- Minor problems may have a cumulative psychological impact.
- Problems of acute illness may be superimposed by physical or mental impairment or economic hardship and social isolation.

Palliative care, which seeks to address are for people at the end of life, and gerontology, which considers the manifestations of and problems associated with ageing, are the two main bodies of knowledge that underpin end-of-life care for the elderly in our society. Both fields of health care have developed in parallel but not until relatively recently in conjunction with each other. Palliative care has only in recent years looked at how to contribute to the care of people with conditions other than cancer and how to work with patients in older age groups; and gerontology has only focused in recent times on healthy ageing, rather than the ultimate life transition that older people make, namely end of life.

Dying choices

An enormous diversity exists in the way people view and approach death and dying. This diversity continues to be evident when people are faced with the knowledge that their own death is approaching. There is no standard, correct or even best way of dying. Yet there is a concept of a "good death", as already touched on in this book. Improving the quality of dying involves recognising that people must be allowed to die in a way that is acceptable to them and is consistent with their beliefs, values and personal family circumstances. Tensions often occur at this point because not only is the person who is dying affected by death, but others also share that experience. Therefore it is the case that communication, discussion and sometimes negotiation and compromise need to take place in the management of individual deaths. Considering how we want to die is not at the forefront of the minds of most of us. We are often too busy living to give it much thought. However, as people grow older thoughts of death and dying increase. Ternestedt and Franklin (2006) claim that there are few studies that shed light on what older people consider to be a good or dignified death. The premise of their study was to search for a deeper understanding of the thoughts and feelings of elderly people regarding how they relate to life when they are close to death. The findings from their study identified three themes: a zest for life; indifference towards living; and a longing for death. A previous study by Seymour (2003) sought to determine what was important to elderly people regarding end-of-life care. The study found that the priorities were: trust, good communication and the ability to evaluate the risks and benefits of individual treatment plans. There was an emphasis on good basic care, appropriate pain management and involvement in decision making.

As discussed previously, there has been a shift in recent decades in the place of death from the community into care homes and hospitals. This has been particularly noticeable in the over 85 age group. Currently the majority of over-75s die in hospital or care homes. The conditions they die from are predominantly the result of complex chronic health problems, often alongside other physical and psychological conditions, so the palliative and end-of-life care needs of this population are particularly discrete. Furthermore, older people's social and family support structures differ from those of younger age groups.

Research evidence about the decisions people make about care at the end of life show that around 75 per cent would prefer to die at home (Higginson and Sen-Gupta, 2000; Luptak, 2006). However there is a clear inverse relationship between the place where people *want* to die and where they *actually* die. This suggests that current service provision varies across the UK and the availability of adequately trained staff for home care is limited. Coupled with this is the concern of the partner or spouse of the dying old person regarding their own ability to cope with caring for them at home. Since a significant proportion of all deaths in the UK are of people aged over 86, it might be expected that they had received end-of-life palliative care. However, palliative care for the elderly is less likely in this population. One reason may be the under-representation of over-65s in hospices and the predominance of care for older people in care homes, where specialist palliative care may not be available. Another factor is that this population are more susceptible to multiple health problems and do not often report their symptoms to doctors (WHO, 2004). The significance of this is that there is inconsistency and a lack of trained professionals in institutions where older people are most likely to die.

The UK Government's recently launched End-of-Life Strategy (see the previous chapter) is designed to support people as they come to the end of their lives, allowing more support for them to die in the setting they choose. It has a particular focus on providing better support and care for those who wish to die at home. This strategy has been welcomed by the organisation Help the Aged.

For older people who may have been in a marriage or partnership for many years, the loss of that partner may have a significant effect. Studies on loneliness in older people identify the death of a partner or spouse as a contributing factor and alert us to the fact that loneliness correlates with negative health outcomes like morbidity and suicide (Waern *et al.*, 2003). Depression has significant consequences for older people and is the most common psychological illness associated with life-threatening disease (Lloyd-Williams, 2003). This is acknowledged by Sheldon (2004) who suggests that when older people who are facing death are confronted by social losses, they distance themselves from their community and their family relationships are affected. The frailty that comes with ageing plus the progression of illness impacts on the older person's ability to maintain social relationships, to maintain roles within the family, and to cope with everyday living.

Dying alone and unsupported can be particularly disturbing for elderly people who are independent and reluctant to be a burden on others. With an increasing number of people choosing to die at home, this brings into sharp relief the role of family and lay care givers in the end-of-life care of the elderly person (Seale and Cartwright, 1994). This is endorsed by Higginson (2003) who proposes that carers' needs should be a priority when end-of-life care decisions are made for seriously ill people who are dying at home.

Elderly suicide

Elderly suicide

Suicide has been discussed earlier in this book from a sociological–cultural perspective (Durkheim, 1951). Despite the fact that suicide, and its prevention, continue to be a priority area for health care in the UK, suicide in the elderly has been a relatively neglected subject, receiving little interest and research attention. Evidence suggests that suicide rates in most industrialised nations increase with age, with the highest rates of all occurring in elderly men. The World Health Organization hold a worldwide Suicide Prevention Day (WHO, 2007). This emphasises that people of all ages commit suicide and that national responses to suicide should meet the needs of the different age groups. The WHO (2007) state that almost 3000 people commit suicide every day and they remind us that the emotional impact on family and friends can last for many years. There is a growing awareness of suicide as a major public health problem, even though it is taboo in many societies, preventing open discussion.

The notion that most elderly suicides are "rational" acts in response to irreversible and understandable situations is not supported by available clinical research. Suicidal behaviour in the elderly is undertaken with greater intent and with greater lethality than by younger age groups. Health- and social-care staff play a vital role in recognising and preventing suicide in this age group (Barraclough,1971; Henriksson, *et al.*, 1995; Conwell, 1997). The role of social isolation as a risk factor for elderly suicide has been identified by Barraclough (1971) who cites "living alone" as the most important social variable. The antecedents, in terms of precipitating life events, appear to be different in the elderly population compared with younger and middle-aged groups. They are associated more closely with interpersonal and relationship problems, financial, legal and occupational difficulties, and less with physical illnesses and other losses.

The role of bereavement is also significant; studies of completed and attempted suicide cite its relevance. Elderly men seem especially vulnerable. Guohua's (1995) study reports a relative risk for widowed men three times greater than that of married elderly males, whereas widowed and married elderly women show similar risk. The first year of widowhood appears to be a particularly vulnerable period.

Although suicide and its prevention remain a significant public health concern, suicide in the elderly still receives little focus in terms of specific preventive strategies or research. This is unfortunate given the established evidence that elderly suicide rates are among the highest, and are in turn more closely related to serious mental illness (especially major depressive illness) and significant physical health problems than in any other group. The situation is compounded by the failed recognition and treatment of those elderly who come into contact with the services. Fundamental to this process is the need to educate health profes-sionals and society in general that the act of suicide in late life is rarely a rational act or an unavoidable tragedy. The graph in Fig. 7.2 (page 106) illustrates suicide trends across age groups in the UK from 2001 to 2006. While there is a little improvement over time for some age groups, this is still an alarming set of data.

In the early 1990s, the highest UK suicide rates were in men aged 75 and over. This age group, however, had the biggest percentage decrease in rates between 1991 and 2006, with those aged 15–44 showing the highest rates since 1997, although the rate in those aged 45–74 was only slightly lower. This pattern was not the same for women: women aged 15–44 had the lowest rates over the same time. Rates for women aged 75 and over had the largest percentage decrease during this period, however, and in 2006 their suicide rate was half that seen in 1991, and only slightly higher than those aged 15–44. For women, the highest suicide rates in 2006 were in those aged 45–74 (National Statistics, 2008). Salib *et al.* (2002) conducted a retrospective analysis of suicide notes obtained from coroners' records of all elderly suicides in Cheshire over a period of 10 years. They provided valuable insights into the thinking of old people before their fatal act. None of the people in this study were known to the psychiatric services. The methods they used were varied, including overdose, hanging or jumping from a height. Salib *et al.* concluded that although only a proportion of elderly suicide victims leave suicide notes, the absence of a note must not be taken to indicate a less serious attempt; many of them are isolated and have no-one to leave a note to, or they have lost the capacity to express themselves.

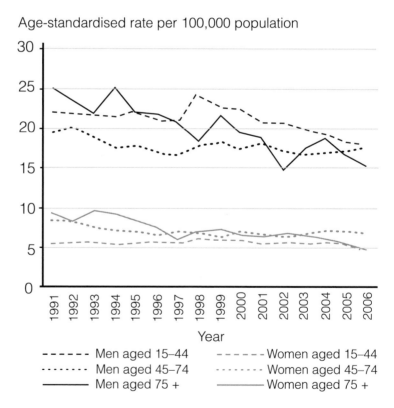

Fig. 7.2 **Trends in suicide in different age groups in the UK from 1991 to 2006**

Death and the challenge of ageing

The National Service Framework for Older People (2001) seeks to promote good mental health in older people and to treat and support those with dementia and depression. It aims to do this by:

- ensuring access to integrated mental health services
- effective diagnosis
- treatment and support for them and their carers.

Services for older people and the primary care services are working to identify ways of enhancing the assessment and clinical management of depression in older people, particularly those with physical illness. The voluntary service providers are also working with other service providers on the resourcing and development of services for vulnerable older people. It is anticipated that the UK Government's new End-of-Life Care strategy will embrace the needs of older people with respect to suicide prevention.

Conclusions

Elderly people have relatively few years left to live, and despite the fact that healthy ageing people are living longer, no treatment – however successful – can significantly extend their life expectancy. There is a view that resource allocation in health care discriminates against this population; philosophers, such as Harris (2005), argue strongly that this discrimination is unfair because elderly people place the same value on living out the remaining years of their lives as young people do. For many old people in Western society, age, illness and social death are inexorably linked and as a society our older people are likely to be sequestered to care homes or nursing homes when their ageing becomes a burden to their families. It is also the case that palliative care or end-of-life care in these institutions is limited and inconsistent across the UK. We know that illness in old age is particularly complex, with single illness conditions being interwoven with other age-related health and psychological conditions. Within the concept of a social death are embedded feelings of loss of role and identity, and fear, loneliness and depression, often coupled with economic hardship. This has led to suicide becoming a significant problem for this population. Within Western society, great value is placed on youth, health and beauty, an ageist view that adds to the sense of worthlessness that some elderly people experience (Devons, 1996). Suicide in the elderly is anticipated to become more prevalent than it is now. It is complex because the risk factors overlap and sometimes are not amenable to change. Some of the key issues are inadequate resources to care for old people at home and formal social care that is restricted to the most needy or those who can fund it privately. The social fabric of our society in terms of neighbourhood and "community spirit" has dwindled over the years, leading to media headlines that describe old people being found in their homes weeks and sometimes months after they have died.

One of the most difficult dilemmas for an older person who is seriously ill involves where they are going to be cared for when they are dying and who will participate in that care. They have a right to be given appropriate information about residential and nursing-home care, hospice in-patient services and care at home, in order to make an informed choice about the end of their life. In reality there is little or no discussion, and they often move into care homes because very little supported home care is available. Moving from their home into care can be a challenge in itself. Action is needed at both an individual and a social level to improve the physical and social health of old people, to reduce the effects of social isolation and loneliness, and to provide treatment and care based on holistic, end-of-life care philosophies wherever they choose to live until they die. They want to live independently and with dignity and with equal access to health and social care, yet the public services across the country are often failing to meet their most basic needs. Therefore education and training for those working in areas of supportive end-of-life or palliative care for the elderly is a priority if high-quality care is to be provided. And palliative care services need to provide flexible and equitable care, that is underpinned by sensitivity to the individual needs of the person, regardless of his or her age.

Reflective questions

1. What are your thoughts on elderly patients being given costly treatments when they are nearing the end of their lives when that money could be spent on the health-care needs of younger people?

2. Consider the following statements about what might constitute a good death. What would you most like for yourself? What are the top three priorities?

- I want to die in my own home.
- I want to die in a hospice, cared for by people who understand how to make me comfortable.
- I want to have someone religious with me at the moment of death, praying for me.
- I would hate to be on public view and want to have privacy.
- I want to die quickly.
- I want the opportunity to say goodbye to my family.
- I would hate to live to be very old.
- I want to live to a good age, as long as I have my faculties.
- I want to die in my sleep and know nothing about it.
- I don't want to die in pain.
- I want to die in solitude.
- I want to be ready when the time comes.
- I want to be with other people on an open hospital ward, and not hidden away.
- I want to be very alert, even if this means being in some pain.
- I want to be ready and accept death when it comes.
- I want to be able to die as the person I am and be accepted for that, even if I am angry or in denial.
- I do not want anyone religious around, nor do I want any religious ideas expressed.
- I want to be able to plan my own funeral.

References and further reading

Barraclough, B. (1971). Suicide in the elderly. In: D.W.K. Kay and A. Walks (eds) *Recent Developments in Psychogeriatrics*. Headley, Royal Medico-Psychological Association, pp. 87–97.

Bennewith, O., Gunnell, D., Kapur, N., *et al.* (2005). Suicide by hanging: a multicentre study based on coroners' records in England. *British Journal of Psychiatry*, 186, 260–61.

Bennewith, O., Hawton, K., Simkin, S., *et al.* (2005). The usefulness of coroners' data on suicides for providing information relevant to prevention. *Suicide and Life-Threatening Behavior*, 35, 607–14.

Cattell, H. and Jolley, D.J. (1995). One hundred cases of suicide in elderly people, *British Journal of Psychiatry*, 166, 451–57.

Conwell, Y. (1997). Management of suicidal behaviour in the elderly. *Psychiatric Clinics of North America*, 20, 667–83.

Department of Health (2008). *National Statistics*. Available at: http://www.statistics.gov.uk/CCI/nugget.asp?ID = 1092&Pos = 6&ColRank = 2&Rank = 1000 (last accessed February 2009).

Devons, C.A.J. (1996). Suicide in the elderly: how to identify and treat patients at risk. *Geriatrics*, 51(3), 67–68.

Durkheim, E. (1951). *Suicide: A study in sociology*. New York, The Free Press (original work published in 1897).

Gunnell, D., Bennewith, O., Hawton, K., Simkin, S. and Kapur, N. (2005). The epidemiology and prevention of suicide by hanging: a systematic review. *International Journal of Epidemiology*, 34, 433–42.

Guohua, L. (1995). The interaction effect of bereavement and sex on the risk of suicide in the elderly: An historical cohort study. *Social Science and Medicine*, 40, 825–28.

Harris, P. (2005). In: M.L. Johnson, V.L. Bengtson, P.G.Coleman and T.B. Kirkwood (2005). *The Cambridge Handbook of Age and Aging*. Cambridge, Cambridge University Press.

Haw, C., Sutton, L., Simkin, S., *et al.* (2004). Suicide by gunshot in the United Kingdom: a review of the literature. *Medicine, Science and the Law*, 44, 295–310.

Hawton, K., Simkin, S., Gunnell, D., *et al.* (2005). A multicentre study of coproxamol poisoning suicides based on coroners' records in England. *British Journal of Clinical Pharmacology*, 59, 207–12.

Henriksson, M.M., Marttunen, M.J., Isometsa, E.T., *et al.* (1995). Mental disorders in elderly suicide. *International Psychogeriatrics*, 7, 275–86.

Higginson, I. (2003). *Priorities and Preferences for End-of-Life Care in England, Scotland and Wales*. London, National Council for Hospice and Specialist Palliative Care.

Higginson, I.J. and Sen-Gupta, G.J. (2000). Place of care in advanced cancer: a qualitative systematic literature review of patient preferences. *Journal of Palliative Medicine*, 3(3), 287–300.

Joseph, J. (1991). Warning. In: S.H. Martz (ed.) *When I am an Old Woman I Shall Wear Purple*. Rhode Island, Papier Mache Press.

Kapur, N., Turnbull, P., Hawton, K., *et al.* (2005). Self-poisoning suicides in England: a multicentre study. *Quarterly Journal of Medicine*, **98**, 589–97.

Kapur, N., Turnbull, P., Hawton, K., Simkin, S., Mackway-Jones, K. and Gunnell, D. (2006). The hospital management of fatal self-poisoning in industrialised countries: an opportunity for suicide prevention? *Suicide and Life-Threatening Behavior*, **36**, 302–12.

Lloyd-Williams, M. (2003). Screening for depression in palliative care. In: M. Lloyd-Williams, M. (ed.) *Pschyosocial Issues in Palliative Care*. Oxford, Oxford University Press.

Luptak, M. (2006). End-of-life care preferences for older adults and family members who care for them. *Journal of Social Work in End-of-Life and Palliative Care*, 2(3), 23–44.

National Statistics (2008). *UK suicide rates continue to fall*. Available at: http://www.statistics.gov.uk/CCI/nugget.asp?ID = 1092&Pos = 6&ColRank = 2&Rank = 1000 (last accessed February 2009).

Salib, E., Crawley, S. and Heeley, R. (2002). The significance of suicide notes in the elderly. *Aging and Mental Health*, 6(2), 186–90.

Savage Landor, W. (2004). *Walter Savage Landor: A Biography*. London, Kessinger.

Seale, C. and Cartwright, A. (1994). *The Year Before Death*. Aldershot, Avesbury.

Seymour, J. (2003). *Technology and the natural death: A study of older people*. Available at: http://www.shef.ac.uk/uni/projects/gop/index.htm (last accessed February 2009).

Sheldon, P. (2004). In: D. Oliviere and B. Monroe (eds) *Death, Dying and Social Differences*. Oxford, Oxford University Press, p.167.

Simkin, S., Hawton, K., Sutton, L., *et al.* (2005). Coproxamol and suicide: preventing the continuing toll of overdose deaths. *Quarterly Journal of Medicine*, **98**, 159–70.

Sutton, L., Hawton, K., Simkin, S., *et al.* (2005). Gunshot suicides in England: a multicentre study based on coroners' records. *Social Psychiatry and Psychiatric Epidemiology*, **40**, 324–28.

Ternestedt, B.M., and Franklin, L. (2006). Ways of relating to death: views of older people resident in nursing homes. *International Journal of Palliative Nursing*, 12(7), 334–40.

Wærn, M., Runeson, S., Allebeck, P., *et al.* (2003). Mental disorder in elderly suicides: A case–control study. *American Journal of Psychiatry*, **159**, 450–55.

World Health Organization (2004). *WHO launches new initiative to address the health needs of a rapidly ageing population*. September 2004. Geneva, WHO. Available at: http://www.who.int/mediacentre/news/releases/2004/pr60/en/print.html (last accessed February 2009).

World Health Organization (2007). *World suicide prevention. Mental health evidence and research*. Geneva, WHO. Available at: http://www.who.int/mediacentre/news/statements/2007/s16/en/print.html (last accessed February 2009).

Chapter 8
Making a case for death education
Dr June L. Leishman

Oh! I have slipped the surly bonds of earth ...
Put out my hand and touched the face of God.

From *High Flight* by John Gillespie Magee, Pilot Officer in No. 412 squadron, killed in action at age 19 (1921–1941)

Introduction

People have been dying since the beginning of time, but the interest in death as a subject of study has only become of significant interest since the 1970s. It was at that time that thanatology flourished in the academic world with the interest resting mainly in the academic domains of psychology, sociology and philosophy. Of course death was covered in medical, nursing and social work curricula, but mainly from a physical care perspective, with little emphasis on what to expect or how to communicate with people near to death.

In addition to the more general academic approach to the study of death, a number of pioneers concentrated on more specific issues. Several, including Jeanne Quint Benoliel (1985), Cicely Saunders, and Elisabeth Kubler-Ross, focused on dying patients and the effects of institutional environments, the process of dying, and pain management as well as the legal, and professional issues concerning death. These courses became a model for others and articulated the need for change in the care of dying people. Benoliel began her pioneering work in death education for care givers by designing a graduate course for nursing students, which she began to teach in 1971. Course topics included social, cultural and psychological conditions that influence death-related attitudes and practices, concepts of grief and ethical and moral issues. However, death education is not taught across all disciplines in health care in ways that are comprehensive and consistent in terms of quality delivery and evaluation.

The motivational driver for producing this book was the June Leishman's own experience of teaching health care students about death and dying in ways that triggered their interest and enthusiasm about the subject and encouraged them to look beyond the procedural aspects of physical care (of course these important aspects of education were also covered).

For many of us death remains a mystery, and for many young people in our developed societies, socialisation – regarding ways of dealing with death on a personal and emotional level – appears to have been unsystematic and ineffective. The world we live in today brings death to our attention on a daily basis. War, terrorism, murder, suicide and issues related to physician-assisted death and euthanasia have become key news issues as we watch television, read newspapers or "surf the net". Coupled with this is the easy access we have to films, computer games and books that have death and dying as their main theme.

The UK Government, in its End-of-Life Care Strategy (2008) has indicated strongly that education and training for health-care professionals is a key priority in providing high-quality care for dying patients and support for their families. It is within these curricula that the broader issues of death and dying will enable health-care professionals to better understand the complexities that come with death and dying. In so doing they will be more able to make sense of the need for effective communication skills in order to talk to patients and their families about dying and death; to be able to assess care needs and plan care thoroughly; to incorporate not only appropriate symptom control but also the important aspects of psychology; to recognise the need for social and spiritual care and be confident to provide this when needed; and to recognise and understand their own beliefs and value systems and how these impinge on and are challenged by the individual beliefs and value systems of people making up the multicultural society we live in.

Much of the literature related to professional education supports this standpoint and highlights the inconsistency and lack of comparability in education and training received by medical, health and social care staff (MacLeod, 2001). This inconsistency is recognised across the disciplines and across the clinical practice areas. Some would suggest that of all health-care professionals, it is nurses who are in the most immediate position to provide care, comfort and counsel at the end of life, as they are at the forefront of care across all age groups and clinical settings. For example, many first-year nursing students encounter their first practical experience with elderly patients, a group in whom death is more likely to occur. Yet they are often ill prepared for dealing with dying patients and their families. It is also a fact that nurses spend far more time with critically ill patients and their families than other care givers. With the (re)domestication and provision of home care in the UK now recognised as a "gold standard", there is increased pressure on community nurses to provide "hands on" practical and palliative care for patients dying at home (McIlfatrick and Curran, 1999; Exley and Allen, 2007). Historically, nurses have been better prepared for this aspect of their professional role than doctors, but a study by Ferrell *et al.* (1999) suggested that end-of-life education for nurses was inconsistent.

Similarly, social workers are major service providers to people who are facing end-of-life issues. They work directly with clients and families and as such death education would be a significant part of their education and training curriculum (Blackman, 1995). Corr (1995) argued that death education should enhance social workers' knowledge and understanding of the subject, and therefore enhance their skills in working with clients and families at this time. The six goals of this type of death education are:

1. To enrich the personal lives of the individuals to whom it is directed by helping them to better understand themselves.

2. To inform and guide individuals in their personal transactions with society by making them aware of services that are available to them as well as their options in dealing with end of life matters such as funeral practices and living wills.

3. To prepare individuals for their public roles as consumers, noting that death is associated with a great number of social issues such as suicide, euthanasia and organ/tissue donation which expand the subject into the realms of public policy, thus making us responsible as citizens for the outcomes.

4. To support individuals in their professional and vocational roles through a high-quality educational programme.

5. To enhance the ability of individuals to communicate effectively about death-related matters.

6. To assist individuals to help clients to appreciate how development across the human life-course interacts with death-related issues.

Building on the works of Saunders, Benoliel and Kubler-Ross, consideration needs to be given to what should be taught to contemporary health- and social-care professionals in order that they are better equipped to cope with death and dying wherever they may encounter it. Consideration also needs to be given to the use of appropriate teaching and learning methods for this complex and challenging subject. Alongside this is the need for a more robust approach to the inclusion of communication skills and spirituality in health and social care education.

Spirituality in death education

Spirituality in death education

Spirituality, put simply, is an eclectic mix of ideas and philosophies that draws on overlapping frameworks of other discourses such as philosophy, religion and metaphysics, among others, as well as the wider social context. It is written into the constitution of hospice and palliative care and is experienced and expressed in many different ways. Before the 1970s spiritual care and religion were closely related and generally provided by chaplains, priests or other faith leaders. However, according to van Hooft (2002) it is still only a minor theme in the literature of medicine, nursing and other health-care professions, largely due to the complexity of the phenomenon. While still the domain of chaplains and faith leaders, over recent years there has been a growing interest in the area across all professional disciplines that involve working with people in need of health and social care. Hamilton (1998) suggests that doctors are best suited to this type of care, whereas others propose that social workers or nurses are best equipped to take on this role. Palliative and hospice care continue to hold the vision of Cicely Saunders (1987), that end-of-life care should apply across the lifespan of the illness, from the time of diagnosis to the end of life, and that it should be multidisciplinary and embrace physical and psychological, as well as social and spiritual, aspects. Cobb (2002) proposes that spiritual care cannot lie outside of the moral compass of health care and that it should be done well and should include some definition of what it is. Cobb also argues that there is an inadequacy of training in spiritual care; in order to respond effectively to the level of need of individual patients spiritual care should be addressed within professional education and embrace the discipline of reflective practice. Modules and courses in spiritual care for nurses and health-care professionals are now more accessible, the forerunner of which in modern times has been offered by the Marie Curie Palliative Care Institute. There is, however, an argument for spiritual care to be covered within areas of health care other than palliative and hospice care, given that the spiritual dimension of humanity is a weighty matter in the face of death, wherever that takes place.

The importance of spirituality is viewed as a key element in recognising the uniqueness of individual people and human benevolence and hope, which can be based on faith of any kind (Seale, 2007). Spiritual care embraces the need for cultural sensitivity and respect for all faith groups and the need to be non-judgemental with respect to different patients and client populations. The marriage of spiritual, physical, social, psychological and cultural domains is the key to providing the model of holistic, client-centred care that Saunders envisioned. Cassidy (1988) says the spirituality of caring "must be the spirituality of the companion, of the friend who walks alongside, helping, sharing, and sometimes just sitting empty-handed, when [they] would rather run away." In addition, the spirituality of caring is "the spirituality of presence, of being alongside, watchful, available of being there". Cassidy also adds: "We who would be a companion to the dying therefore must enter into their darkness, go with them at least part of the way, along their lonely and frightening road, enter into the suffering and share in some small way their pain, confusion and desolation".

When considering how to incorporate spiritual care into professional education, questions regarding what knowledge attitudes and skills are needed to practice spiritual care are raised. How should it be taught, learned and assessed? And how do we measure quality in spiritual care? Given the complex nature of spirituality and the duality of abstract concepts and concrete experience that constitutes spiritual care, it is proposed that experiential learning and reflective practice would feature significantly in any spiritual care curriculum (Kolb, 1993). Mitchell (2005) believes that the keys to good spiritual and cultural care for those at the end of their life are good communication, being comfortable in engaging with patients and their family, and being self aware.

Communicating and counselling in death education

**Communi-
cating and
counselling**

Communication skills are at the core of health care. Good communication allows patients and families an opportunity to understand and reflect on their situation and make decisions that are appropriate and relevant to their needs. It would be fair to say that all education programmes for health professionals include communication skills and some communication and counselling skills. However, the business of communication, particularly with people facing death or the bereaved, is often fraught with difficulty.

The consultation between patient and heath-care professional, as Kleinman (1980) notes, is a transaction between lay and professional < explanatory models >. It is also a transaction separated by differences in power at both a social and a symbolic level. However, despite this its main function is to address the issues of health concern for the patient, and to translate these concerns into understandings, from which a treatment or care regimen can be developed that is acceptable to both the patient and the health-care professional. It is possible, however, in this transactional process to forget about cultural, age and gender differences that exist between the patient and the health-care professional, as well as individual differences in their health beliefs (Giger and Davidhizar, 1991).

It is also important to recognise that communication is not something that occurs just between the health-care professional and the patient. People closely associated with the dying person and those who care for that person may also be included in this transactional process. Payne and Ellis-Hill (2001) identify terms used to describe the same group of individuals whose involvement with a dying person differs in regard to their social relationship with that person. These are:

- carers
- care givers
- care takers
- informal carers
- companions
- relatives
- family
- friends
- significant others
- next of kin
- visitors.

Health-care professionals will be required to communicate with any or some of the above depending on the role they play in the dying person's life. Harding and Higginson (2003) state that providing information and education is the most common type of communication delivered to carers. Iconomou *et al.* (2001) identified the high rates of anxiety and depression among carers, and suggest that psychological support should be provided in the form of counselling. It is evident therefore that communication skills are very important in this field and one of the most challenging aspects is actually telling a person that they are dying.

In a paper on breaking bad news, Buckman (1984) gave one reason why doctors find it difficult to talk to patients about death: that is, they have their own fears about illness and death and sometimes view death as a "taboo subject". Baile *et al.* (2005) agree that breaking bad news is a complex communication task and it is frequently stressful. Bad news is commonly defined as anything that negatively alters an individual's view of himself or herself as a person, or any information that adversely affects an individual's view of his or her future. Diagnosis of terminal illness certainly sits in that category – challenging views about being healthy, having a future and how one is perceived by others. The meaning of any bad news, like death and dying, is individual – a thread that has run through this book from the outset. As such, any communication with someone that communicates bad news has to be personalised to that person. However despite the difficulties faced by people who have to communicate bad news to patients, the majority of dying people do want information about their condition, their chances of cure, or their future demise (Meredith *et al.*, 1998). This is affirmed by Rodriguez *et al.* (2006) who looked at implicit and explicit language used by oncologists in communication with their patients.

Communication with patients already features in the undergraduate core curricula for medical and nursing and allied health-care professional education (General Medical Council, 2003; Becket and Maynard, 2005; Hafford-Letchfield, 2006; Longley *et al.*, 2007). However it is up to the individual educational institution to design curricula that meet these core components. Key elements to communicating effectively with patients and their families is the skill of carefully listening to the patient's experience, beliefs and reaction to news and imparting information that maps clearly to the patient's circumstances and needs. The capacity of bad news to completely change and negatively transform someone, at least initially, is one of the main reasons that it is so difficult to do. Faulkner's book for health professionals (Faulkner, 1998) provides a list of dos and don'ts for giving bad news to patients (Table 8.1).

Table 8.1 **The dos and don'ts of breaking bad news**
(adapted from Faulkner, 1998)

DOs

> **Do** check if the patient wishes anyone else to be present
>
> **Do** check the patient's understanding of what you are saying
>
> **Do** clear enough time
>
> **Do** control any potential interruptions
>
> **Do** follow the patient's agenda
>
> **Do** have all the facts to hand
>
> **Do** negotiate time for conversations and take notes if necessary

Do observe and acknowledge the patient's emotional state and reactions

Do stop if the patient indicates that they do not wish to continue

DON'Ts

Don't answer questions unless you have all the facts to hand

Don't block emotional expressions from the patient

Don't break bad news to the patient's relatives before telling the patient him or herself

Don't decide what is most important for the patient

Don't give inappropriate reassurances

Don't give too much information at any one time

Don't hurry any communication

Don't make assumptions about the impact of the news readiness to hear the news, who else should be present or the patient's priorities or level of understanding

Don't use euphemisms like "a little ulcer" if it is a cancerous tumour

---

Recognising the importance of communication skills and the relevance of spiritual care, we should now consider the whole concept of death education for professionals working with clients across a range of settings and with different client populations. Hillier and Wee (2001) believe that this significantly important aspect of health care should form part of early education and training curricula across all health-care disciplines. Magnani *et al.* (2002) share Hillier and Wee's view (2001) that this thread should run through undergraduate education and into postgraduate study because most people who die will have some contact with different health-care professionals; they also believe that all health-care professionals should experience palliative care education at an interdisciplinary level wherever possible. Bunn *et al.* (2008) agrees that end-of-life care must be incorporated into nurse education and throughout continuing professional development.

Thus it can be conceded that historically no health-care

professions have received extensive or appropriate education on caring for dying patients and their families. This has impacted on the inconsistent quality of care provision in this area. The subject has largely been avoided or addressed only in a limited fashion because of its sensitive nature and/or a lack of appropriately qualified and capable individuals to teach the subject (Alchin, 2006). However, provision for end-of-life care is improving within professional health-care education and training curricula (Dickinson, 2007). It works most successfully when the educators are in a position to theoretically underpin the study of death across the range of disciplines with an approach that makes death a feature of the human condition, and when students are encouraged to reflect on the theories, their own beliefs and value systems and gain insights through enquiry-based, experiential learning. With the introduction of the Gold Standards Framework (2001), the Liverpool Care Pathway (Foster *et al.*, 2003) and more recently in 2008 by the Government's End-of-Life Care Strategy we should see further developments in this area.

A model for death education

A model for death education

To deliver education about death, dying and bereavement effectively, the complex body of knowledge of the subject needs to be made clear to students. It is proposed that this involves understanding of five key areas of knowledge (Table 8.2). However, these five areas of knowledge need to be taught and learned within a conceptual framework that embraces the key domains given in Table 8.3 on page 124.

In addition to the content and context of delivery, it is important how this sensitive and challenging subject area should be taught and assessed. There should be a combination of traditional theoretical delivery and experiences from clinical practice, coupled with evaluations of case studies, plus discussions, role play, narrative analyses, the use of a range of media, genre and the arts, reflective exercises and self-evaluation. There is an increasing interest in the use of creative arts in palliative and end-of-life care as a means of exploring the feelings and thoughts of the dying person (Mayo, 1996). However, despite

Table 8.2 **The five key areas of knowledge**

1. Dying process	Physical, psychosocial and spiritual experience of facing death, living with terminal illness and dying
	Managing pain and caring for the terminally ill and dying
2. Decision making for end of life	Aspects of life-threatening illness and terminal illness that involve choices and decisions about actions to be taken, for individuals, their families and professionals
3. Loss, grief and bereavement	Physical, behavioural, cognitive and social experience of and reactions to loss, the grieving process and practices surrounding grief and loss
	Communication and counselling skills for delivering bad news, working with the dying and the bereaved
4. Assessment and interventions	Information gathered, decisions made and actions taken by professionals to determine and/or provide for the needs of the dying, their loved ones and the bereaved
	Recognising and understanding the impact of technology on human life
5. Traumatic death	Sudden, violent, inflicted and/or intentional death or shocking encounters with death

the recognition that working with dying patients and their families is challenging, very little is written about the use of creative arts in education of health-care professionals. There are many ways beyond the lecture that can enhance teaching, learning and assessing death and dying education. Poetry, art, films, television and literature give us glimpses of the world through other people's eyes and facilitate more creative thinking about complex, emotional and challenging issues. On almost every day there will be some television programme that has addresses death and dying in one way or another; it may be a news report about a war situation, a terrorist attack, a murder or the escalating culture of violence among young people. Or it may be a popular ongoing drama series, a film or a documentary.

When we look at fiction, we are faced with the same menu of death by many different authors. Death and dying is all around us.

Table 8.3 **The domains of death**

Historical perspectives	Historical context and historical changes affecting the death experience, and the theoretical paradigms in the field of thanatology up to the 1970s
Religious and spiritual	Relationship between religious and spiritual belief systems and the reaction to and coping with death
Cultural and socialisation	Influence of cultural, ethnic and social parameters on the experience of death and loss
Larger systems	Social organisations beyond the individual and family that affect the experience of dying, death and grief
Family and individual	Social, cognitive and physical encounters and interpretations of dying, death and loss from the standpoint of the person, and the group of people with a relational bond and long-term commitment who define themselves as "family"
Life span	Consideration of death and dying and develop mental perspectives from infancy to old age
Contemporary perspectives	Theoretical perspectives on death and dying and the factors that influenced them from the 1970s to the present day
Professional issues	Factors affecting professionals[']' training, abilities and responsibilities in providing care
Resources and research	Materials, organisations and groups of individuals who facilitate knowledge acquisition (ideas and materials based upon the findings of empirical research and theoretical synthesis add to the knowledge base)
Ethical and legal	Aspects of dying, death and/or loss related generally to determining right from wrong and specifically to the principles of medical ethics
	Legal issues refer to the articulated laws of a society as they pertain to thanatology

Therefore making use of what is readily available in our teaching makes sense. Specially selected contemporary films, current television programmes and poetry by known authors provide a different approach to teaching and learning in this area. They also bring sensitive and complex issues, such as suicide, other voluntary deaths, trauma and inflicted death into the educational arena; they are not easy topics to deal with for either the lecturer or the student. The use of these media as teaching and learning tools can be undertaken individually by the learner as a reflective exercise, in student groups as a critical discussion session, or as preparation for a lecture or tutorial. In this book, for example, each chapter has a piece of poetry or prose that presents an expression of death, dying or loss as perceived by one person. Each has a story to tell, and each can be interpreted by the reader in ways that are meaningful for them. Adopting creative ways of learning can enrich discussion and debate, encourage reflection and analysis, and assist in sensitively dealing with challenging issues. Examples of other media that are useful in this way are given in Table 8.4.

Table 8.4

Examples of media genre and art that may be used to generate discussion in teaching and learning about death and dying

Feature films

Four Weddings and a Funeral	Shows the depth of the passion and pain of the bereaved and mourners
Bringing Out The Dead	Explores the impact of loss for people who are professionally involved with death and dying
Truly, Madly, Deeply	Focuses on the pain and loss throughout the mourning of a loved one [note forms]
The Bucket List	Life-affirming adventures of two men from different cultural backgrounds who assist one another during their terminal cancer

Television programmes

House	The episode "Informed Consent" depicts a cancer victim with fluid in his lungs who is adamant that he wants to die
Holby City	Everyday experiences of health-care professionals

Poetry

To an Athlete Dying Young (A.E. Houseman)	Presents death as a celebration of a young life lived to its fullest.
Ariel and *The Bell Jar* (Sylvia Plath)	Plath, one of the most influential poets of the 20th century, pours out the troubling emotions that led to her suicide in 1963

Teaching should include opportunities for invited speakers, service users and, possibly, chaplains, faith leaders, counsellors and other agencies to discuss their role with the dying person and their family. Finally, and importantly, addressing the way in which these courses of study are evaluated must be ongoing in order to improve and develop the curriculum and maintain its currency in an ever-changing society.

Because of its complexity, this is not something that can, or should, be taught in a few short hours. The preferred option is for death education to be a thread that flows logically through a programme of study from the very first year until completion of the course. Of course, this may not be possible; for some professionals, carefully selected short, continued professional development courses or modules of study may be all that is available. The main aim of death education is to contribute to the specific education of those who, as a result of personal or professional circumstances, are closely associated with dying, death or bereavement. Within this aim is the desire to facilitate personal development, self-awareness and reflection in the learner as they gain knowledge and understanding about a fundamental and pervasive aspect of human experience – death. Thus a carefully crafted programme that weaves research-orientated theoretical study with enquiry-based, ethically and legally focused learning that includes meaningful group work discussions and reflective exercises would help to achieve this goal. Death can be fearful and anxiety-provoking for many people, including those who work with the dying. Studying death can also raise fear and anxiety in students. It is important when teaching this subject to be aware of this and to build into the programme time for student support.

Conclusions

There is a concerted effort to educate nurses and other health-care professionals in end-of-life, although limited progress has been made in evaluating the provision of death education across the health-care education sector. The challenge of achieving an overall objective evaluation of educational outcomes remains. State-of-the-art death-related content needs to be reflected in the educational curricula for all professionals and at all levels. In enhancing depth of knowledge and understanding about death and dying, those in caring roles will be more able to rise to the challenges that dying brings to their engagement with people of all ages and cultures. It will also equip them to look more thoughtfully at the complexities of how people die, beyond the realms of clinical environments. This chapter has tried to make a case for death education playing a key part in health-care professionals curricula in ways that have not been undertaken previously with any consistency. With advances in technologies, teaching, learning and assessment strategies can draw on contemporary pedagogies to meet the needs of anyone whose work involves death, dying and supporting the bereaved. Ways in which education can reach people in the modern world are diverse and there is no reason why people in the most remote regions of our nations should not be able to access high-quality education in this important field.

Reflective questions

1. Why do you think that nursing and medical educational institutions have traditionally offered very little death education?

2. List three things you think dying patients can teach us about death and dying and say why?

3. Reflect on one film, novel or television programme about death or dying. Is there a particular scene that has stayed with you and helped you think differently about loss, death and bereavement?

4. Think about *how* you have learned about death and dying in your own life. What has that learning taught you about your own beliefs and values?

5. How do you think understanding more about the complexities of death and dying will help you as a practitioner?

6. Write your own "bucket list" of ten things that you would want to do or achieve before you die. For each one say why it is important to you.

References and further reading

Alchin, N. (2006). *Theory of Knowledge.* Hodder Murray, New York.

Avery, G. and Reynolds, K. (2000). *Representations of Childhood Death.* Basingstoke, Macmillan.

Baile, W.F., Buckman, R., Schapira, L. and Parker, P.A. (2005). Breaking bad news: more than just guidelines. *Journal of Clinical Oncology*, 24(19), 3217.

Becket, C. and Maynard, A. (2005). *Values and Ethics in Social Work.* London, Sage.

Benoliel, J.Q. (1971). Assessments of loss and grief. *Journal of Thanatology*, 1, 182–94.

Benoliel, J.Q. (1974). Anticipatory grief in physicians and nurses. In: B. Schoenberg, A.C. Carr, A.H. Kutscher, D. Peretz, and I.K. Goldberg (eds) *Anticipatory Grief.* New York, Columbia University Press, 218–28.

Benoliel, J.Q. (1985). Loss and adaptation: Circumstances, contingencies, and consequences. *Death Studies*, 9, 217–33.

Blackman, R.A. (1995). Helping the terminally ill face death with dignity. *Quality Letter March*, 7(2), 19–23.

Buckman, R.A. (1984). Breaking bad news: Why is it still so difficult? *British Medical Journal*, 288, 1597–99.

Bunn, F., Dickinson, A., Barnett-Page, E., McInnes E. and Horton, K. (2008). A systematic review of older people's perceptions of facilitators and barriers to participation in falls-prevention interventions. *Ageing and Society*, 28(4), 449–72.

Cassidy, S. (1988). *Sharing the darkness. The Spirituality of Caring.* London, Darron, Longman and Todd, pp. 55.

Cobb, M. (2002). *The Dying Soul: Spiritual Care and the End of Life.* Buckingham, Open University Press.

Corby, B. (2006). *Applying Research in Social Work.* Maidenhead, Oxford University Press.

Corr, C.A. (1995). Death Education for Adults. In: I.B. Corless, B.B. Germino and M.A. Pittman (eds). *A Challenge for Living: Dying, Death and Bereavement.* Boston, Jones and Bartlett.

Dickinson, G.E., Clark, D. and Sque, M. (2007). Palliative care and end of life issues in UK pre-registration, undergraduate nursing programmes. *Nurse Education Today*, 28(2), 268–70.

Du Boulay, A. (1994). *Cicely Saunders. The founder of the modern hospice movement.* London, Hodder and Stoughton.

Exley, C. and Allen, D. (2007). A critical examination of home care: End-of-life care as an illustrative case. *Social Science and Medicine*, 65, 2317–27.

Faulkner, A. (1998). *When the News is Bad: A Guide for Health Professionals.* London, Nelson Thornes.

Ferrell, B.R., Grant, M. and Virani, R. (1999). Strengthening nursing education to improve end-of-life care. *Nursing Outlook*, 47, 252–56.

Foster, A., Rosser, E., Kendel, M. and Barrow, K. (2003). Implementing the Liverpool Care Pathway (LCP) In hospital, hospice, community and nursing home. In: J. Ellershaw and S. Wilkinson (eds) *Care of the Dying: A Pathway to Excellence*. Oxford, Oxford University Press.

General Medical Council (2003). *Tomorrow's doctors: Recommendations on undergraduate medical education*. Available at: http://www.gmc-uk.org/education/undergraduate/GMC_tomorrows_doctors.pdf www.gmc-uk.org (last accessed February 2009).

Giger, J.N. and Davidhizar, R.E. (1991). *Transcultural Nursing*. St Louis, MO, Mosby Year Book.

Gold Standards Framework (2001). *A programme for community palliative care NHS end of life care programme*. Available at: http://www.goldstandardsframe-work.nhs.uk (last accessed February 2009).

Hafford-Letchfield, T. (2006). *Management and Organisations in Social Work*. Exeter, Learning Matters.

Hamilton, N.G., Edwards, P.J., Boehnlein, J.K. and Hamilton, C.A. (1998). The doctor-patient relationship and assisted suicide. *American Journal of Forensic Psychiatry*, 19, 59–75.

Harding, R. and Higginson, I.L. (2003). What is the best way to help care givers in cancer and palliative care? A systematic literature review of interventions and their effectiveness. *Palliative Medicine*, 17, 63–75.

Hillier, R. and Wee, B. (2001). From cradle to grave: palliative medicine education in the UK. *Journal of the Royal Society of Medicine* 94(9), 468–71.

Iconomou, G., Vaginakis, A.G., and Kalofonos, H.P. (2001). The informal needs, satisfaction with communication, and psychological status of primary care givers of cancer patients receiving chemotherapy. *Supportive Care in Cancer*, 9, 591–61.

Kleinman, A. (1980). *Patients and Healers in the Context of Culture*. California, University of California Press.

Kolb, D.A. (1993). The process of experiential learning. In: M. Thorpe, R. Edwards, and A. Hanson (eds). *Culture and Process of Adult Learning*. London, Routledge.

Kubler-Ross, E. (1969). *On Death and Dying*. New York, MacMillan.

Li, S. (2004). Symbiotic niceness: constructing a therapeutic relationship in palliative care settings. *Social Science and Medicine*, 58(12), 2571–83.

Longley, M., Shaw, C. and Dolan, G. (2007). *Nursing towards 2015: Alternative scenarios for healthcare, nursing and nurse education in the UK in 2015*. Nursing and Midwifery Council. Available at: http://www.nmc-uk.org/aFrameDisplay.aspx?DocumentID=3349 (last accessed February 2009).

Macleod, J. (2001). *Qualitative Research in Counselling and Psychotherapy*. London, Sage.

Magnani, J.W., Minor, M.A., Aldrich, J.M. (2002). Care at the End of Life, *Academic Medicine*. May 2002, 77, 4.

Mayo, S. (1996). Symbol, metaphor and story. The function of group art therapy in palliative care. *Palliative Medicine*, 10(3), 209–16.

McIlfatrick, S. and Curran, C. (1999). District nurses' constructions of quality in providing palliative care. *Journal of Advanced Nursing*, 31(4), 775–82.

McLean, L. and Williamson, L. (2007). *Impairment and Disability: Law and Ethics at the Beginning and End of Life*. Abingdon, Routledge.

Meredith, C., Symonds, P., Webster, I., *et al.* (1998). Information needs of cancer patients in the West of Scotland: A cross sectional survey of patients' views. *British Medical Journal*, 313, 724–31.

Mims, C.A. (2000). *When We Die: The Science, Culture and Rituals of Death*. St Martin's, Griffin.

Mitchell, G.K. (2005). How well do General Practitioners deliver palliative care? A systematic review. *Palliative Medicine*, 16(6), 457–64.

Noys, B. (2005). *The Culture of Death*. Oxford, Berg.

Payne, S. and Ellis-Hill, C. (2001). *Chronic and Terminal Illness: New Perspectives in Caring and Carers*. Oxford, Oxford University Press.

Robertson, S., Kendrick, K. and Brown, A. (2003). *Spirituality and the Practice of Heath Care*. Basingstoke, Palgrave Macmillan.

Rodriguez, T., Malvezzi, M., Chatenous, N., Bosetti, C., Levi, F. and La Vecchia, C. (2006). Trends in mortality from coronary heart and cerebrovascular diseases in the Americas: 1970–2000. *Heart*, 92, 453–60.

Saunders, C. (1987). What's in a name? *Palliative Medicine*, 1, 57–61.

Scutton, S. (1995). *Bereavement and Grief: Supporting Older People Through Loss*. London, Arnold.

Seale, C. (2007). *Constructing Death: The Sociology of Dying and Bereavement*. New York, Cambridge University Press.

Taylor, S. and Field, D. (2007). *Sociology of Health and Health Care*. Oxford, Blackwell Publication.

Thomas, R. S. (1955). *Collected Poems 1945–1990*. London, Phoenix, Orion Publishing Group.

Van Hooft, S. (2002). *Towards a Philosophy of Caring and Spirituality for a Secular Age, Spirituality and Palliative Care*. Melbourne, Oxford University Press, pp. 38–50.

Vincent, J. A., Phillipson, C. and Downes, M. (2006). *The Futures of Old Age*. London, Sage.

Walter, T. (1999). *On Bereavement: The Culture of Grief*. Buckingham, Open University Press.

Ward, B. (1996). *Good Grief: Exploring Feelings, Loss and Death with Over Elevens and Adults: A Holistic Approach*. Philadelphia, Jessica Kingsley Publishing.

Woods, S. (2007). *Death's Dominion: Ethics at the End of Life*. Maidenhead, Open University Press.

Chapter 9
The end
June L. Leishman

Now when I was a young man I carried me pack
And I lived the free life of the rover.
Then in 1915, my country said, 'Son,
It's time you stop ramblin', there's work to be done.
'So they gave me a tin hat, and they gave me a gun,
And they marched me away to the war.
And the band played 'Waltzing Matilda,
As the ship pulled away from the quay,
And amidst all the cheers, the flag waving, and tears,
We sailed off for Gallipoli.

From *And the Band Played Waltzing Matilda* by Eric Bogle (1972)

Throughout this book, the message has been that death is all around us and is part of us. It is not only present where illness limits life. It is present in the everyday world we live in. Only this week we have seen yet more horrific pictures on our television screens and newspaper front covers of people dying as a result of wars, conflict, atrocities, natural disasters and other non-illness related death. As with the other chapters in this book, this final chapter invites the reader to consider the lyrics written by Eric Bogle, a high-school dropout, sometime accountant and former singer in a Beatles-style band, who emigrated from Scotland to Australia in search of money and adventure. In 1971, with Australia embroiled in Vietnam alongside the United States, Bogle sat down to write what would become one of the most admired songs about war *And the Band Played Waltzing Matilda*.

Protest songs seem to have existed forever and there are many more that could be cited here from singer–songwriters such as

Perspectives on death and dying

Joan Baez, Bob Dylan and Paul Simon. In this song Bogle chose to tackle current events of the 1970s by exploring historical events as far back as Australia's first real test on the battlefield, in Gallipoli, Turkey in 1915, just 14 years after the Commonwealth of Australia was born. The meaning behind the lyrics still resonates today where war and the numbers of young men and women dying in conflicts across the world is significant. The collateral damage resulting from these conflicts affects our own society and every other society where these actions take place, at an individual, national and global level. Not only are armed forces at risk, but the innocent also perish. The late 20th and early 21st century has witnessed a raft of worldwide terrorist attacks, wars and conflict leading to the death of vast numbers of people, young and old, serving forces personnel and ordinary citizens. And all of these are brought to out attention, often as they are occurring, through modern information technology. Similarly millions of people around the world are killed as a result of natural disasters such as hurricanes, earthquakes and tsunami, demonstrating the fragility of life and the force of the elements of the planet on which we live.

"Looking back to the future" like Bogle in his version of *Waltzing Matilda*, this book encourages readers to look at death and dying today, starting from a social history–anthropological–sociological premise. Death and dying, as experienced and understood over the centuries, has been drawn to the reader's attention. The book has explored the medical health care aspects of death and dying, and has introduced readers to developments in care, medicine and health care over time. Alongside this, and very importantly (given the numbers of diverse cultural groupings in modern Britain), has been discussion of cultural differences and concerns about people seeking refuge in the UK who are held in detention camps. In recognising diversity, issues related to gender and age difference have also been included.

Allan Kellehear, in his work *A Social History of Dying*, Kellehear (2007) reminds us that Stone-Age people had an idea of death, but not of dying. Death came so suddenly and violently there was not a passage of time over which people slipped from one world to the next. The central idea underlying this book has been that the passing of time brings with it changing beliefs, values and understandings that are contextualised within their own historical frame. Thus we have moved from accepting death as part of everyday life, through medicalising and sequestering death and (it seems for some) back again to accepting death – albeit accepting in a different way. It is evident that even today, some people in the modern world consider discussions about the nature of dying as taboo.

As society changes, the way in which the dying are cared for has also evolved over time. We have moved from familial and lay caring to professional technical caring and holistic caring, although not always in a directly linear way. And as ways of dying and caring for those at the end of their life have progressed over the years, the arrival of "slow deaths" has transformed the ways in which people prepare for death and how professionals care for them through their death trajectory. This book makes a case for a broader, more robust approach to education and training of health-care professionals at all levels in death education, and suggests that alongside the clinical medical and nursing knowledge and skills needed for caring for the dying, there is significant merit to be had from thinking "out of the box" on this hugely complex, highly personal and challenging topic. This book has touched on controversial issues such as suicide and euthanasia and the use of organs and tissues following death, and has given readers an opportunity to reflect on key issues covered in each chapter. The use of poems and prose and the meaning behind them allow us to look at these issues through the eyes and minds of others.

There is so much more to this complex, fascinating and important topic, and it is hoped this book will inspire readers to look at the subject through different eyes and see the challenges and opportunities that understanding more about this human condition can bring.

References

Kellehear, A. (2007). *A Social History of Dying.* Cambridge, Cambridge University Press.

Perspectives on death and dying

Index